THE EMPIRE

By Graham McNeill

CONTENTS

Produced by Games Workshop

© Copyright Games Workshop Limited 2006. The Double-Headed/Imperial Eagle device,
the Games Workshop logo, Games Workshop, Warhammer, Balthasar Gelt, Emperor Karl Franz, Flagellant, Grand Theogonist Volkmar,
Greatsword, Helblaster Volley Gun, Helstorm Rocket Battery, Knights of the Blazing Sun, Knights Panther, Knights of the White Wolf, Kurt Helborg,
Ludwig Schwarzhelm, Luthor Huss, Mordheim, Old World, Reiksguard, Skaven, Steam Tank, Sigmar and all associated marks, logos, places, names,
creatures, races and race insignia/devices/logos/symbols, vehicles, locations, weapons, units, characters, products, illustrations and images
from the Warhammer world and Warhammer 40,000 universe are either ®, TM and/or © Games Workshop Ltd. 2000-2006,
variably registered in the UK and other countries around the world. All Rights Reserved.

British Cataloguing-in-Publication Data. A catalogue record for this book is available from the British Library.
Pictures are used for illustrative purposes only.

Certain Citadel products may be dangerous if used incorrectly and Games Workshop does not recommend them for
use by children under the age of 16 without adult supervision. Whatever your age, be careful when using glues,
bladed equipment and sprays and make sure that you read and follow the instructions on the packaging.

Re-printed December 2008

ISBN: 1-84154-799-9   www.games-workshop.com   **Product code: 60 03 02 02 002**

INTRODUCTION

The Empire is a vast land of Men that fights for its survival with each passing day. Ruled over by the Emperor Karl Franz, the discipline and martial skill of its armies is renowned throughout the Old World. This book is the definitive guide to collecting, painting and playing with an Empire army in games of Warhammer.

The Warhammer Game

The Warhammer rulebook contains the rules you need to fight battles with your Citadel miniatures. Every army has its own book that works with these rules and allows you to turn your collection of miniatures into a battle-ready force. This particular army book describes the stalwart Men of the Empire, their army list and the miniatures you can collect.

Why Collect an Empire Army?

The Empire's armies are made up of disciplined, professional soldiers, heroic knights and mighty war machines. Though many of the foes of the Empire boast warriors stronger and more powerful than Humans, none can doubt the ingenuity or tenacity of an Empire soldier on the battlefield.

An Empire army will often contain a wide array of different troop types, from the seasoned warriors of state regiments and Knightly Orders, to mighty Great Cannons and crazed Flagellants. You can choose an Empire army that marches into the teeth of the enemy with halberds lowered or one that blasts its foes from afar with powerful artillery and volleys of handgun fire – or anything in between!

How This Book Works

Every army book is split into four main sections that deal with different aspects of the army. Warhammer Armies: The Empire contains:

The Empire. The first section introduces the Men of the Empire and their deeds in the Warhammer world. It covers the most pivotal times of the Empire and the bloody wars that have forged it into the most powerful nation of the Old World.

Forces of the Empire. Every unit type in the Empire army is examined here. You will find a full description, alongside complete rules and details of any unique abilities they possess.

The Empire Army List. The army list takes all of the warriors presented in the previous section and arranges them so you can choose an army for your games. Units are classed as either Characters, Core

Units, Special Units or Rare Units and can be taken in different quantities depending on the size of game you are playing. Each unit also has a points value to help ensure you can you pit your army against an opponent's in a fair match.

The Empire Army. In the final section you will see photographs of the range of Citadel miniatures available for the Empire army, gloriously painted by Games Workshop's 'Eavy Metal team. Colour schemes for the different provinces of the Empire and example armies can all be found in this section.

Find Out More

While Warhammer Armies: The Empire contains everything you need to play a game with your army, there are always more tactics to use, different battles to fight and painting ideas to try out. The monthly magazine White Dwarf contains articles about all aspects of the Warhammer game and hobby, and you can find articles specific to the Empire on our web site:

www.games-workshop.com

THE EMPIRE

Over centuries of war, the Empire has grown to become a vast realm of provinces and city-states, bound together under the rule of the Emperor. It is the most powerful nation in the Old World, stretching from the borders of Bretonnia in the west to the sweeping plains of Kislev in the east. Its borders encompass vast forests, towering mountains and prosperous, cosmopolitan cities of universities and culture, where the arts of war and science go hand in hand. Yet it is also a dangerous, brooding land of superstition and fear, where peasants clutch talismans to ward off evil and the corrupting power of Chaos. Since its founding by the legendary warrior king Sigmar, the Empire has endured invasions, plagues and civil wars, triumphing over all through the courage of its armies and the steadfastness of its people. However, evil still lurks in the depths of the land, festering in the darkness beneath the mountains and growing in ancient forest strongholds. Orcs raid the Empire's borders and the threat of invasion from the northern tribes who worship the monstrous Chaos gods is an ever-present danger.

Such threats must be faced and defeated by the Emperor's armies, professional state troops raised and trained by the Elector Counts. Disciplined regiments of Halberdiers and Spearmen march into battle alongside dashing Swordsmen, their advance covered by the fire of Handgunners and Crossbowmen. The courage and discipline of these soldiers is renowned throughout the Old World, and there are few foes that can break the steadfast ranks of a well-led Empire army. As well as these state troops, the Emperor can call upon the expertise of the Imperial Gunnery School of Nuln, whose mighty Great Cannons and Mortars blast the foe from afar. The fearsome Battle Wizards of the Colleges of Magic destroy the Emperor's enemies with powerful spells, and heavily armoured horsemen of the Knightly Orders crush their foes beneath their thunderous charges. The Imperial College of Engineers provides the Emperor's armies with deadly experimental creations, such as the terrifying Helblaster Volley Guns, the armoured Steam Tanks and deadly Rocket Batteries.

The year is 2522 and the Empire is ruled over by the Emperor Karl Franz. The Empire's peril has never been greater as sinister Chaos cults plot in the cities, Beastman warbands stir in the forests and old enemies look enviously across its borders. In such times of war and bloodshed, it is the armies of the Empire that form the bastion against these unrelenting dangers and the coming of the End Times.

SIGMAR'S REALM

The nation that would grow to become the Empire took its first fledgling steps two and a half thousand years ago, and much of what is known of it comes from the Dwarf records of the time. The long wars between the Dwarfs and Elves were over; the Dwarfs retreated to their mountain holds in the Worlds Edge Mountains and the Elves abandoned their colonies, crossing the sea back to Ulthuan. Though the Dwarfs remained, their influence was much weakened, for many of their most powerful kings were dead and their holds overrun. When the mountains of the east erupted in flames and were riven by mighty earthquakes, the power of the Dwarfs was finally broken and a new enemy was to rise in strength and ambition – Orcs and Goblins.

Hordes of greenskins poured across the Worlds Edge Mountains, through the passes previously guarded by Dwarf fortresses, to ravage the lands west of the mountains. As the Dwarf realm reeled from the never-ending attacks of Orcs and Goblins, many Human tribes began migrating southwards: Unberogens, Teutogens, Thuringians, Cherusens, Norsii and Merogens to name but a few. Fighting in common cause against the greenskins, it is certain that both Dwarfs and Men quickly recognised great potential in the other. The Dwarfs saw allies who could help them win back their lost empire, and Men were eager to learn the secrets of metalworking and the means of forging strong weapons of iron. These tribes were a far cry from the civilised Men of the Empire today; clad in rough furs, they dwelt in mud huts and carried crude weapons of stone or bronze. The Dwarf records tell that these men were fierce and courageous, battling the hordes of Orcs and Goblins for possession of the dark forests. The mightiest of these Men was known as Sigmar, the first son of the Unberogen chieftain, and a twin-tailed comet blazing across the sky heralded his auspicious birth. Sigmar was a warrior of great nobility and strength, and by his fifteenth year he had already fought scores of battles against the greenskins.

The Heldenhammer

The Orcs and Goblins grew more cunning and in one daring attack captured Kurgan Ironbeard, High King of the Dwarfs, as well as several members of his household as they made their way to the Grey Mountains. As fate would have it, Sigmar and his most trusted warriors were already hunting this band of Orcs and caught them in the deep forest before they could escape. Sigmar slew many Orcs that day, burning their foul corpses on a huge pyre after freeing the Dwarf captives. In gratitude for his release, King Kurgan presented Sigmar with a magical heirloom of his family, a magnificent rune-forged warhammer named Ghal Maraz, which means

Skull Splitter. Sigmar accepted the King's generous gift and the two warriors pledged to aid one another in the wars against the rampaging greenskins.

The wars against the Orcs and Goblins continued for many years and the bond between Men and Dwarfs became stronger as the threat from the east grew. Seven years later, upon the death of his father, Sigmar became chieftain of the Unberogen and set about uniting the Human tribes of the west through brutal conquest and exceptional cunning. Sigmar was a powerful and charismatic leader, but above all he had a vision: a land united under his rule, free of Orcs and Goblins, governed by fair laws and protected by a strong, disciplined army. After years of brutal war and diplomacy, twelve of the great tribes of Men had sworn mighty oaths to follow Sigmar and, together with his Dwarf allies, he drove the greenskin scourge from the lands west of the Worlds Edge Mountains, earning himself the name Heldenhammer, meaning Hammer of the Goblins.

The few Human tribes who still opposed Sigmar were driven south into the inhospitable Grey Mountains or, like the Norsii, north beyond the Middle Mountains, leaving Sigmar the undisputed ruler of the lands between the Worlds Edge Mountains and the Great Ocean. Thus when the Dwarfs were once again threatened by hordes of Orcs and Goblins, King Kurgan despatched the Runesmith Alaric the Mad to seek aid from Sigmar and the race of Men.

Black Fire Pass

As soon as he heard of the danger to the Dwarfs', Sigmar called a gathering of chieftains and ordered them to muster their warriors. He marched this army into the Worlds Edge Mountains to join his forces with those of King Kurgan. A vast horde of Orcs and Goblins was pushing through Black Fire Pass, the only route by which an army could hope to cross the Black Mountains. Many battles have since been fought at this crossing point, but this battle eclipses all others. The vastly outnumbered armies of Men and Dwarfs stood side by side against the greenskins as they poured up the valley, but Sigmar and King Kurgan had chosen the field of battle with great cunning. Their armies were drawn up where the pass was at its narrowest, where the overwhelming hordes of Orcs and Goblins could be faced on an equal footing. The battle lasted for many brutal hours, with the howling green tide breaking time and time again against an unbending line of splintered shields and bloody blades. As well as Sigmar, great heroes such as Ulfdar the Berserker, Marbad of the Endals and Queen Freya of the Asoborns made their names that grim day, their deeds becoming the stuff of legend for generations to come.

As the Orc line fell back in disarray for the final time, Sigmar led a fearsome charge deep into the enemy ranks. With howls of victory, he and his fellow chieftains cut a swathe through the fleeing greenskins and slaughtered them without mercy. In recognition of this incredible victory, Sigmar was pronounced Emperor of all the lands between the Grey Mountains in the south and the Middle Mountains in the north. King Kurgan presented Sigmar with a magnificent crown and the two monarchs swore eternal fealty to one another. In gratitude for Sigmar's aid in saving the Dwarf realms, King Kurgan commanded Alaric the Mad to begin the long process of creating twelve magical swords known as Runefangs, one for each of the tribal chieftains of the new Emperor's realm.

The Age of Sigmar

Fifteen years after his rescue of King Kurgan, Sigmar was crowned Emperor. His coronation marks the beginning of the Imperial calendar and the first day of the Empire. He ruled justly and courageously from his capital, Reikdorf (later to be renamed Altdorf), granting land to the twelve tribal chieftains who had sworn allegiance to him and aided him in his many wars. These divisions were based upon the old tribal territories and the chieftains who ruled these provinces took the title of count. Sigmar ruled the

Empire for another fifty years and during this time the rough villages blossomed into small towns, the people multiplied, and many new settlements were founded. Of course there were still enemies to fight. Marauding Goblins continued to cross over the Worlds Edge Mountains, and there were plenty of savage Human tribes in the northern forests beyond the Middle Mountains that raided the fledgling Empire.

Little else is known of Sigmar's reign, for the Dwarf annals are concerned chiefly with their own affairs and Sigmar's part in them. All that is known for certain is that Sigmar eventually put aside his crown and journeyed eastwards, supposedly to Karaz-a-Karak to meet his old friend Kurgan Ironbeard. If he ever arrived at that most famous of Dwarf holds the records do not tell. The time of Sigmar passed, and he became a legend, the heroic forebear of his people. Temples and shrines were built to his memory, and a cult grew up to venerate him as the Empire's founder. Within a generation Sigmar was openly worshipped as a god, with his own priesthood headed by a Grand Theogonist, Johann Helsturm. The Cult of Sigmar became one of the most powerful faiths in the land, with many thousands of loyal followers, and the hero of Black Fire Pass took his place alongside the old gods of the Empire.

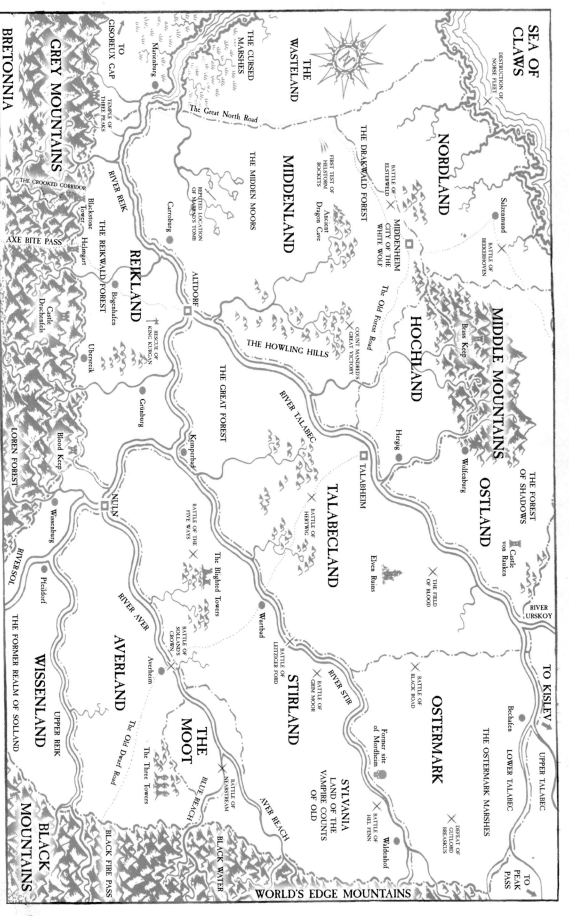

GEOGRAPHICAL MAP OF THE EMPIRE

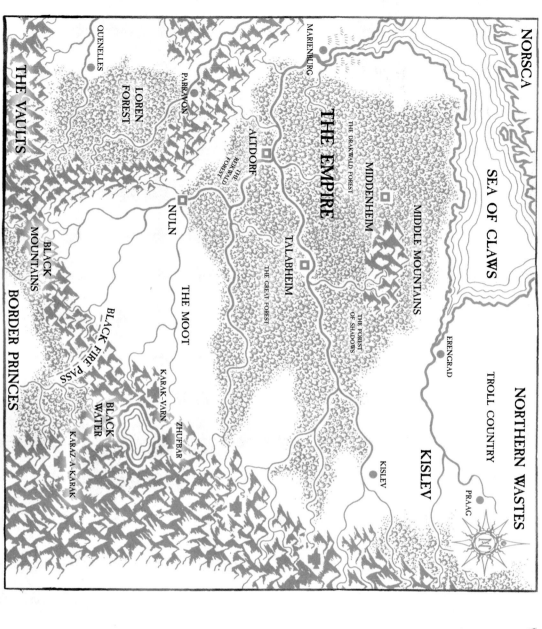

NORSCA

SEA OF CLAWS

NORTHERN WASTES

TROLL COUNTRY

KISLEV

PRAAG

ERENGRAD

KISLEV

MARIENBURG

THE DRAKWALD FOREST

MIDDENHEIM

MIDDLE MOUNTAINS

THE FOREST OF SHADOWS

THE EMPIRE

ALTDORF

THE REIKWALD FOREST

TALABHEIM

THE GREAT FOREST

NULN

THE MOOT

PARRAVON

LOREN FOREST

QUENELLES

THE VAULTS

BLACK MOUNTAINS

BORDER PRINCES

BLACK FIRE PASS

BLACK WATER

KARAZ-A-KARAK

KARAK-VARN

ZHUFBAR

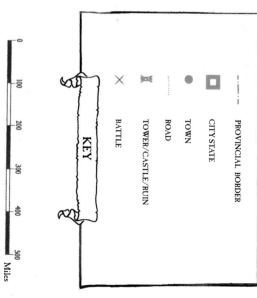

KEY

- - -	PROVINCIAL BORDER
☐	CITY STATE
●	TOWN
⋯	ROAD
⚒	TOWER/CASTLE/RUIN
✕	BATTLE

0 100 200 300 400 500 Miles

THE WARHAMMER WORLD

NAGGAROTH DARK ELF LANDS

LUSTRIA

ULTHUAN ELVEN KINGDOMS

REALM OF CHAOS

ALBION

SEA OF CHAOS

NORSCA

ARABY

THE SOUTH-LANDS

THE DARK LANDS

THE EMPIRE

THE STEPPES

THE UNKNOWN LANDS

TO CATHAY

THE AGE OF THE EMPIRE

With Sigmar's passing, it was feared that destructive wars would erupt between the counts he left behind, but instead of fighting to see who should rule, the counts gathered at Reikdorf to decide what should be done. After much tense deliberation, the counts swore that they would hold true to Sigmar's vision and that a new Emperor would be elected from among their number. The counts became known as Elector Counts and thus the Empire's system of elected Emperors was established, surviving in one form or another to the present day. The land of Sigmar grew and prospered under the leadership of the Elector Counts and the armies of the Empire fought their enemies with the courage and ingenuity for which Sigmar's heirs had earned a well-deserved reputation.

The Skaven Wars

As the centuries passed and the Empire continued to grow in power, Emperors came and went; some good, some bad, but none of such infamy as the hated Boris Goldgather. During his grossly incompetent rule, the people starved, the armies were neglected and many border forts were left virtually unmanned. In this weakened, dispirited condition, the Empire was in no state to weather the greatest catastrophe ever to strike the Old World – the Black Plague of 1111. Tens of thousands died over the winter of that year, entire villages and towns wiped out as the virulent disease spread throughout the Empire with unnatural rapidity. The dead quickly outnumbered the living, and by the time the plague began to subside, fully three quarters of the Empire's population were rotting in open mass graves. The only good thing to come of the plague was that it claimed the life of Boris Goldgather, who died in his castle surrounded by fretting apothecaries (none of whom, it is believed, tried *too* hard to save him).

Without an Emperor, even one as incompetent as Boris, the Empire was at its most vulnerable. The loathsome ratmen, the Skaven, erupted from hidden tunnels beneath the earth, looting and destroying wherever the plague they had unleashed had done its evil work. Thousands were slaughtered or enslaved, but those that remained fought back bravely under the inspired leadership of the Count of Middenheim, Count Mandred – later known as the Ratslayer. Mandred rallied the surviving Elector Counts and led an army of his countrymen against the Skaven, fighting a series of bloody battles throughout the devastated towns and blighted landscape of the Empire. The ratmen were finally driven from the Empire at the Battle of the Howling Hills, where Mandred himself beheaded the verminous Warlord at the head of the Skaven army with one stroke of his Runefang. Following the battle, Mandred had

the warlord's skull fashioned into a helmet of terrifying aspect that would forever live in the darkest nightmares of the ratmen.

An Empire Divided

The Empire recovered rapidly from the Skaven wars, largely thanks to the death of Boris Goldgather and the dynamic leadership of the newly elected Emperor Mandred. His respected generalship and charismatic personality held the Empire together, but with its population virtually wiped out, many villages were simply abandoned, and much of the Empire was left deserted. Tragically, Emperor Mandred's life (and the Empire's recovery) was ended upon the envenomed blade of a Skaven assassin, and in the years following this calamity, the electoral system of the Empire began to fall apart.

Personal rivalries, conflicting ambitions and simple jealousy divided the Elector Counts and they failed to reach a decision as to who should become the new Emperor. Blood was shed in the Grand Throne Room of the Graf of Middenheim when these squabbles turned violent and the counts returned to their lands with anger in their hearts. In 1360, Ottilia, the Elector Countess of Talabecland, proclaimed herself Empress and declared war upon her rival, the Elector Count of Stirland. In the years that followed, the Imperial crown passed between the Elector Counts as the Empire broke apart into separate warring states. The next few hundred years saw a succession of Emperors as one pretender after another launched a claim to the throne, and the Empire was riven by bitter civil wars and strife. During these turbulent times there were two Emperors – the elected Emperor and the Elector Count of Talabecland who continued to claim hereditary position as Emperor following the self-appointed reign of Ottilia. To make matters worse, in 1547, Count Siegfried of Middenland took it upon himself to declare himself Emperor as well, marking the beginning of the Time of Three Emperors, with each claimant soliciting allies and supporters amongst the other provinces.

The provinces themselves now became more or less ungovernable, and for the next century and a half, the Elector Counts fought rivals and rebellions within their own lands as well as their many enemies from without. The final straw came when the infant Countess Magritta of Marienburg was elected Empress and the Grand Theogonist of Sigmar himself refused to acknowledge the appointment. For all intents and purposes, the Empire ceased to exist as a unified nation under an Emperor. With Sigmar's people divided into petty, squabbling fiefdoms, the Empire was easy prey and its enemies gathered like carrion eaters around a corpse.

THE CRUSADES

Though the majority of Knightly Orders are sworn to the protection of the Empire and its people, there are still times when they find themselves bound for war in far-off foreign lands. When Sultan Jaffar of Araby invaded the lands of Estalia, the king of Bretonnia (at that time Louis the Righteous), raised a mighty army and pledged to free the land from the oppressor's grasp. The Bretonnian King issued a call to arms to all warriors of honour and the Grand Masters of many Empire Knightly Orders pledged themselves to this noble cause, seeking to prove their valour in wars beyond the civil strife engulfing the Empire. During the bloody Crusades that followed not only was Estalia freed, but the knights took the war to Araby itself to destroy the Sultan's empire. The knights were filled with merciless zeal and they tore down the Sultan's decadent palaces, burned thousands of tomes in his library and cast down the idols from his temples.

The Destruction of Solland

Gorbad Ironclaw, one of the most feared Orc warlords of his day, arose to command a vast horde of Orcs and Goblins, and led his armies through Black Fire Pass to devastate the provinces of Averland and Solland. Eldred, Count of Solland, marched his forces to the River Aver, where he commanded the crossing beyond Averheim. Gorbad's army plunged into the river and attacked the defenders on the opposite bank. Though the greenskin horde lost thousands of warriors crossing the river, the Orcs gained a foothold on the riverbank.

This was the beginning of the end for the defenders, for their only hope had been to hold the Orcs on the far bank. The Imperial army found itself becoming encircled and Eldred desperately sought to quit the field of battle before his men were slaughtered. But Eldred's decision came too late, for Gorbad had despatched his cavalry to attack the Halfling realm of the Moot further north and circle around behind the Empire army.

As Eldred's personal bodyguard battled to protect their lord, Goblin wolf riders and Orcs on vicious boars rode over the horizon to flank the Empire army. Within moments, a disciplined withdrawal had turned into a rout and, knowing that the day was lost, Eldred led his Greatswords into the swirling mêlée to face the leader of the Orcs. Resplendent in his long silver cloak and glittering crown, the last Elector Count of Solland faced the terrifying form of Gorbad Ironclaw in single-combat. Gorbad was monstrously huge, and even armed with a mighty Runefang, Eldred was no match for the warlord and was brutally cut down. The Elector Count's body was dismembered and hung upon the Orc warlord's trophy racks. Gorbad captured Eldred's Runefang and took his crown as the spoils of war, and the battle became known by the few survivors as the Battle of Solland's Crown.

Gorbad's invasion was ultimately defeated at the Siege of Altdorf (though not before the elected Emperor Sigismund was brutally torn apart by a wyvern) and his army scattered as winter set in. The threat to the Empire from Gorbad Ironclaw was ended, though the province of Solland was utterly destroyed, and its lord's Runefang lost. The areas of land it had once encompassed were subsumed into the province of Wissenland and its name and history passed into memory. It was feared that the legendary sword of Alaric the Mad was lost forever but, centuries later, a warrior band led by the Dwarf Thane Ergrim Stonehammer rediscovered the lost blade deep in the lair of a mutated beast in the Worlds Edge Mountains. Stonehammer fought the creature, smashing its skull with one blow of his runic hammer and recovered the Runefang from its treasure horde. He returned to the Empire and presented the Runefang to the Prince of Altdorf and, though the province of Solland no longer existed, the return of the ancient weapon was greeted with great celebration. Without an Elector Count of Solland to wield the newly returned Runefang, the sword was kept in the Imperial Treasury – to be presented to the greatest of heroes and wielded in battle in times of dire need.

The Wars of the Vampire Counts

As the Time of Three Emperors dragged on with no sign of any of the claimants achieving superiority, a dreadful threat was stirring in the cold shadow of the Worlds Edge Mountains. Sylvania, the most ill-famed region of the Empire, had long been shunned by all right-thinking folk, but its infamy truly began when Vlad von Carstein, a vampire, wrested control of the province from the previous Elector Count, Otto von Drak. Many of the other noble families objected to the thought of having an outsider rule them, but these dissidents were quickly silenced, and under Vlad's iron grip, the province of Sylvania prospered. The other Elector Counts looked on with indifference at the changes, too caught up in their own power struggles to pay much attention to such a backward province. For the next two hundred years, Vlad ruled over Sylvania under the guise of different identities to prevent anyone becoming aware of his undying nature. In 2010, judging the Empire to be at its weakest, Vlad launched his bid to become the immortal Vampire Emperor.

Marching at the head of the Sylvanian army and a host of undead, Vlad invaded Stirland and laid waste to the Ostermark before turning his attention to the heart of the Empire. For the next forty years, Vlad's armies ravaged the land until he eventually fought his way to Altdorf, seat of Prince Ludwig, one of the claimants to the title of Emperor. The siege lasted many months, but in the Empire's darkest hour the Grand Theogonist, Wilhelm III, seized Vlad in a desperate grip and bore him from the city walls, impaling them both on the stakes at the base of the wall. With Vlad gone, much of the Sylvanian army began to disintegrate and the surviving Vampires were forced to retreat. Prince Ludwig marshalled his forces to give pursuit, but fearful that the victory would give his bid for the throne more credence, his rivals united against him and the pernicious lords of Sylvania were given time to regroup and regain their strength. Years later, Konrad von Carstein emerged as Vlad's successor and launched another invasion of

---

PROVINCES OF THE EMPIRE

Though the Empire is often spoken of as a united nation, this is not truly the case. It is a vast land of individual and extremely independent states, joined together by ties of culture, religion, language and common interests. Today, these states are of two distinct kinds: city-states and provinces. Originally there were only what are now called provinces, but over the years the largest cities have grown in importance and have become self-governing. The borders of these provinces were based upon the ancient tribal homelands and over the centuries the boundaries have changed, with new states emerging and others disappearing. The cursed land of Sylvania, long haunted by the dread Vampire Counts, was once a province of
great importance, but is now a backward region ruled by the count of Stirland and shunned by all sane folk. Solland is no more than memory now, for it never recovered from the destruction wrought by the Orc warlord Gorbad Ironclaw. Each of the surviving provinces is fiercely proud of its heritage and there are many idiosyncrasies and dialects that vary from province to province. Those of the east and north are generally more rustic and belligerent, having lived under the shadow of invasion for most of their existence, whereas those in the west and south are considered more cosmopolitan and 'civilised' (or effete and snobbish, depending on who you ask).

the Empire. So great was his insane viciousness that the three claimants to the Imperial throne were forced to ally against him, and he too was defeated, cut down by the Dwarf hero Grufbad and Helmar (the soon to be Count of Marienburg) at the Battle of Grim Moor in 2121.

The last and most dangerous of the Vampire Counts was Mannfred, a subtle, devious and treacherous individual. He allowed the various contenders for the Imperial throne to think that with Konrad's death, the Sylvanian threat was over and waited for them to fall upon one another again. When the Empire was once more wracked by civil war Mannfred attacked, his undead legions marching through the snows towards Altdorf and defeating the hastily assembled armies sent to stop him. Mannfred's force reached Altdorf in late winter and he arrived to find the city undefended. Triumph filled Mannfred until the Grand Theogonist, Kurt III, appeared on the battlements and began to recite the Great Spell of Unbinding. Seeing many of his followers crumbling to dust, Mannfred ordered a hasty retreat. After an abortive attack on Marienburg, the Count was driven back to Sylvania, where the Imperial nobles put aside their differences and invaded Sylvania in an attempt to end the threat of the vampires once and for all. Eventually, Mannfred was brought to battle at Hel Fenn in 2145 where Prince Martin of Stirland cut him down. For his heroic feat the Count of Stirland claimed all of Sylvania and thus were ended the Vampire Wars, though the threat of the Vampire Counts' return ensures that none dare forget the dread of this shadow-haunted land. Though ostensibly part of Stirland, Sylvania is, in reality, an abandoned province where the dead are easily stirred from their slumber and the dark forests are still haunted by unspeakable horrors that prowl the night.

The Great War Against Chaos

As the land of Sigmar was riven with invasions and destructive, internecine wars, the power of the dark gods was growing stronger in the Chaos Wastes of the far north. The Chaos Wastes are a nightmarish landscape of raw magical energy inhabited by all manner of diabolical creatures and bloodthirsty tribes that worship the vile gods of Chaos. When the tides of magic flow strongly, these followers of Chaos pour south into the land of Kislev, slaughtering all in their path. In the winter of 2301, the Chaos warlord Asavar Kul rose amongst the tribes of the north and launched an attack into Kislev. The Empire remembers this invasion as the Great War Against Chaos. An army of Kislevites and Ostlanders mustered to face Kul and his allies, but it was massacred north of Praag, and the horde of monsters, Daemons, beasts and marauders advanced along the western foothills of the Worlds Edge Mountains. The Chaos army fought and destroyed a contingent of Kislevites defending the last bridges of the River Lynsk and Kul's forces crossed the last barrier between it and the city of Praag.

The Siege of Praag lasted throughout the spring and summer, with the city's brave defenders hurling back their attackers time and time again with desperate heroics and stalwart bravery. But as winter set in and the year drew to a close, Praag fell and the hordes of Chaos ran amok. The raw power of Chaos engulfed the city and Praag was changed forever, its survivors fused together in hellish and inhuman shapes. Living bodies melted into the walls of the city itself, so that it became impossible to tell flesh from stone. Distorted faces peered from walls, agonised limbs writhed from the pavements, and pillars of stone groaned with voices that issued from once Human lips. Praag had become a living nightmare and a grim warning of the suffering that lay ahead if the warriors of the Dark Gods were victorious.

Magnus the Pious

As the Empire readied itself for full scale invasion, a leader arose from the horror of these troubled times: Magnus, a noble of Nuln. He would later become known as Magnus the Pious due to his unflinching faith in Sigmar and his belief in the idea of a unified nation. Magnus was a magnificent orator whose rousing speeches raised a massive following among the common folk of the Empire. He marched northwards from city to city, addressing the people in the market places, gathering about him an army the likes of which had not been seen for an age. The Elector Counts were shrewd politicians and recognised Magnus as a powerful leader, quickly realising that they could gain much prestige by supporting him. Soon provincial troops and the soldiers of the Elector Counts marched alongside the citizen militia, and by the time the army reached Middenheim it was the largest single force that had ever been assembled in the history of the Empire. Magnus was forced to divide his troops into two armies, as no single place could provide enough food and water to support all of them.

The first army, consisting mostly of vengeful Kislevite lancers and glory-hungry knights, rode with all speed to Praag in the hope of relieving the siege. These warriors discovered the horror that Praag had become and quickly turned south to wreak their vengeance upon the Chaos horde. Magnus marched his second army to the city of Kislev itself, hoping to resupply at the capital before continuing onwards. While travelling north, the army was joined by Teclis, greatest of the High Elf mages, who had travelled from the island of Ulthuan and now pledged his incredible powers to Magnus' cause. Upon reaching Kislev, Magnus discovered the city already under bloody siege by Asavar Kul's army of the Dark Gods, with but a few Kislevites and a contingent of Dwarfs from Karaz-a-Karak desperately fighting to defend it. The city could not hold much longer and Magnus knew that if Kislev fell, the Empire would be next.

Marching in the ranks of the common soldiers, Magnus immediately ordered the charge, and his enemies were scattered by this sudden attack. Grim-faced regiments of state troops drove a wedge deep within the Chaos host, supported by hails of crossbow bolts and thunderous volleys of handgun fire. Victory seemed assured, but Asavar Kul was a mighty leader, and rallied his warriors and used their greater numbers to encircle Magnus' army. Horrifying Daemons slaughtered entire regiments with razor talons and brazen, spell-forged blades while evil sorcerers unleashed powerful, ancient magic. Teclis and the Human wizards he had recently trained fought against the sorcery of Kul's shamans in a magical battle that burned the skies with lethal energies. Magnus' army was surrounded and it seemed that the fate of the Old World was sealed.

As Kul's warriors fell upon Magnus' army in the final attack, the Kislevite lancers and Imperial knights returning from Praag appeared over the ridge of what would become known as the Hill of Heroes and thundered into their enemies with hatred burning in their hearts. The Dwarfs and remaining defenders charged from the city and Magnus seized this last, desperate chance to lead the Men of the Empire forward in glorious battle. The Chaos hordes faltered as they suddenly faced no less than three armies. The Kislevites were driven to wild fury by the destruction wrought upon their beloved land, and the host of Asavar Kul was slaughtered by the implacable anger of the combined forces. The army of Chaos was shattered and thousands of its warriors were hacked down as they turned to flee in utter rout. The Old World had been saved.

MORDHEIM, CITY OF THE DAMNED

Mordheim was once the greatest city of the Ostermark, but corruption and madness ran riot within its walls as the second millennium since Sigmar's coronation drew to a close. A twin-tailed comet appeared in the sky on the first day of the year, growing ever closer as the final day of the millennium approached. A depraved festival atmosphere grew in the city, and it is said that Daemons crept from the shadows, crying joyously and cavorting with man and woman alike. As the clocks struck midnight, the comet smashed down upon the city like a hammer from the heavens. Sigmar had judged Mordheim lacking and those unfortunates who survived mutated and died in withering agony. Mordheim had become the City of the Damned, cursed forever to be a place of ill fortune and misery until its eventual destruction at the hands of the Grand Theogonist and a combined force of Knightly Orders.

The Empire Endures

Following this historic victory, the people of the Empire demanded that Magnus be elected Emperor and the Elector Counts had no choice but to accede to this. In 2304, Magnus was crowned Emperor and immediately set about restoring order to the provinces of the Empire, hunting down the servants of Chaos in the forests, and resettling many wild and long-abandoned lands. Magnus knew that if the Empire was to survive it needed order and the help of its new allies, and thus one of Magnus' first acts was to ask Teclis to help him create an institution whereby wizards might be properly trained. Teclis' companions advised the great mage against such a course, claiming that the secret sorceries of the Elves were not meant for Men, but Teclis realised that the safety of the whole world rested upon the folk of the Empire, and so he agreed to Magnus' request. Following this, the Colleges of Magic were established in the city of Altdorf under the protection of the Prince of that city, and Teclis taught the first Masters and laid down the laws by which they were to study before he returned to the Elven Kingdoms of Ulthuan.

Magnus also recognised the valuable contributions the master gunners of Nuln and the Engineers of Altdorf had made to the defence of the Empire. He granted them formal charter and for ever more both institutions would proudly bear the prefix 'Imperial' and would become integral parts of the Emperor's armies. Magnus proved to be an extremely capable Emperor and when he died the Imperial crown passed without incident to Count Leopold of Stirland, and subsequently to his grandson Dieter.

The reign of Dieter IV was extremely unpopular and he was universally loathed by the people of the Empire. Dieter was eventually deposed in 2429 following the scandal of his collusion with the Burgomeisters of Marienburg. In return for a huge donation to the Imperial coffers, Dieter had allowed the city-port of Marienburg to secede from the Empire. Wilhelm III, the Prince of Altdorf and Elector Count of the Reikland was elected the new Emperor and since his accession, the crown has remained with the Princes of Altdorf through wars and times of great upheaval all the way to the present Emperor, Karl Franz.

THE LAND OF THE EMPIRE

The Empire is the greatest realm of the Old World, stretching from the icy Sea of Claws in the north to the soaring Black Mountains in the south. To the west, the Grey Mountains form the Empire's border with the noble kingdom of Bretonnia, while its eastern frontier is the virtually impenetrable wall of the Worlds Edge Mountains and the cold steppes of Kislev. Within its extensive borders can be found gloomy, tangled forests, where brigands, greenskins and Beastmen make their lairs in forgotten Elven ruins and ancient fortresses clinging to towering spires of rock. The Empire is a land of savage, primal magnificence, but it is also a land of danger and peril where death and war are never far away.

The Towering Mountains

The great natural barriers of the mountains both protect the Empire from invaders and harbour some of its most dangerous foes. The three main ranges of mountains – the Worlds Edge Mountains, the Grey Mountains and the Black Mountains – converge in the far south of the Empire in a high, soaring land known as the Vaults. Orcs and Goblins, Skaven and unspeakable horrors of Chaos infest the great caverns and tunnels of these ranges and their malign gaze is ever turned towards the Empire.

The Worlds Edge Mountains are grimly forbidding peaks, tall beyond imagining and seeming to scrape the sky with their immensity. In ancient times, the entirety of the mountains was once the domain of the Dwarfs, who crafted vast cities and fortresses into the rock. Grand processional tunnels once linked the halls of their underground realm, stretching from the far north to the south beyond the Old World itself. At various strategic points the tunnels branched east and west to hidden gates in the mountainsides, allowing passage from one side to the other. When the Dwarf realm fell into ruin, many of these tunnels and halls were destroyed, forgotten or captured by Night Goblins and other creatures of evil. Only the insanely brave or foolhardy would dare risk the untold dangers of crossing beneath the mountains, but even the overland routes are incredibly dangerous. In 2520 Engineer Gerhart attempted the first aerial crossing of the mountains in his 'heavier than air' vessel, a refinement of Engineer Rauvork's Phantasmagorial Aerial Splendiferousness Enabler. Whether or not he succeeded is unknown as he has yet to return…

The passes that cross these inhospitable peaks are rife with Goblin tribes and Trolls, but if an invading army wishes to cross the mountains, these are the only possible routes. Mighty fortresses of ingenious design

ALTDORF
SEAT OF THE EMPEROR

The home of Emperor Karl Franz, Altdorf has been the Imperial capital since the accession of Wilhelm III. Altdorf is a bustling city with a substantial community of traders and fortune seekers from all across the Old World. It is also the centre of magical lore and its eight Colleges of Magic are famous throughout the Old World and beyond. The city stands astride the confluence of the rivers Reik and Talabec, and is renowned for the numerous bridges that traverse these waterways. Many of these bridges have been designed by the College of Engineers, equipped with hissing steam-driven pistons that raise and lower them in all manner of unusual ways, allowing ships to travel further up the Reik. However, as is always the way with contraptions designed by the engineers, they can be somewhat temperamental and often activate when least expected – a fact the current Emperor is well acquainted with after his infamous dunking in 2518. The city is also renowned as a seat of learning and the University of Altdorf is the most highly respected academic institution in the Empire, where lords and princes from many lands come to sit at the feet of the foremost thinkers in the Old World.

MIDDENHEIM
CITY OF THE WHITE WOLF

This great and impregnable fortress stands atop the Ulricsberg, a sheer-sided pinnacle of white rock that rears from the surrounding forest like the fang of a great wolf. Four wide highways built on towering viaducts climb from the forest floor and provide the main access to the city. Wooden drawbridges connect the city gates with these highways, and these can be raised to isolate the city in times of war or plague. In addition there are numerous cranes, chairlifts and rope ladders, which are used to pull goods (and sometimes people) up the side of the cliffs. The Ulricsberg is riddled with tunnels, ancient tombs and catacombs but, after several incidents involving mutants and Skaven, access to them is strictly forbidden. From Middenheim's many tall towers it is possible to look out over the Great Forest to the south and the Drakwald to the west. Middenheim is known as the City of the White Wolf, the symbol of the god Ulric, patron deity of the city. The Temple of Ulric stands within the city of Middenheim, making it the centre of his cult throughout the Old World.

defend these strategic points, most of which are of ancient Dwarf construction and have known constant battle for thousands of years. Many of these fortresses are now manned by soldiers of the Empire, the Dwarfs having retreated to their few surviving holds in the distant reaches of the Worlds Edge Mountains.

In the north of the Worlds Edge Mountains is Peak Pass, which cuts through to the Desolation of Drakenmoor. Overlooked by orc tribes living in the ruins of Karak Ungor and Gnashrak's lair, it is a perilous crossing for those foolish or desperate enough to travel eastwards out of the Empire. In recent times, it has been noted as the site of several great battles between the Dwarf Slayer King of Karak Kadrin and the Kurgan hordes of Vardek Crom.

Though Peak Pass has gained some infamy in recent years, the greatest of all the passes over the mountains is where the Worlds Edge Mountains and Black Mountains divide – Black Fire Pass. This deep cleft in the rock is famous throughout the Empire as the site of Sigmar's great victory against the Orcs, which saw him crowned Emperor. The steep sides of the pass, sheer walls of dark, menacing rock, rise above the track below, widening out in the middle of its length into a massive upland valley that remains littered with the rusted blades and bleached bones from the countless battles that have been fought here.

To the west, the Grey Mountains divide the Empire from Bretonnia, realm of the Knights of King Leoncoeur. Like the Worlds Edge Mountains, there are Dwarf settlements within the mountains, but these are fewer in number and far less wealthy than the mighty holds of the east. The Grey Mountains have an evil reputation with the folk of the southern Empire, its shadow-haunted crags the source of many a dark legend. Whispered tales are told of corpses of villagers drained of blood and the reoccupation of Blood Keep, legendary home to a Vampire warrior order. Macabre storytellers delight in telling of the bleak and forbidding Castle Drachenfels, a haunted ruin said to once have been the lair of a powerful necromancer.

Most of the passes across the Grey Mountains are narrow and dangerous, wide enough for small groups or a train of horses, but not much else. Bretonnian and Imperial fortresses guard the few large passes through the Grey Mountains, the widest of which lies to the southwest of Altdorf and is known as Axe Bite Pass. The eastern end of this pass is protected by the fortress of Helmgart, a massive tower that rises steeply from the mountainside and whose battlements overlook the path below. On the far side lies the Bretonnia castle of Montfort, and both have seen much fighting over the centuries, as ambitious Imperial nobles and Bretonnian knights seek to gain an advantage over their neighbours. The short-lived crusade of Baugard the Rash of Parravon in 2512 (to avenge an insult done to his infamously ugly wife by the visiting Count of Averland) ended before the walls of Helmgart when his knights were bloodily repulsed by the keep's massed cannons.

NULN

Nuln is at the heart of the Empire's southern trade routes, where travellers from Wissenland, Stirland, Averland and further east converge. In previous times, Nuln was home to the court of the Emperor, though its reputation as a seat of learning has since been overshadowed by Altdorf in the last few centuries. Nuln is the home of the Imperial Gunnery School, a sprawling network of forges where veteran gunsmiths manufacture and maintain the Imperial artillery trains. Steam-powered air pumps (developed by the Dwarfs for circulating fresh air to deep mines below the mountains) are fitted throughout the entire complex to vent the acrid fumes of the blazing foundries, and portions of Nuln are forever wreathed in palls of choking black smoke. North of Nuln, the Reik is too wide to bridge, and the great bridge at Nuln is one of the great marvels of the Old World. Though there are bridges at Altdorf (where the Reik divides into a number of lesser channels) it is a point of some pride in Nuln that none of the capital's bridges can be said to span the entire width of the mighty Reik.

The northern tip of the Grey Mountains gradually declines into a hilly upland region known as the Gisoreux Gap – the principal route between Bretonnia and the Empire – though many merchants and nobles prefer to risk the journey across the mountains rather than add weeks to their travels.

There are other ways across the mountains, smaller routes and forgotten paths that may be traversed freely throughout the summer months. The ambitious but overconfident Goblin warboss Fizgit the Sneaker attempted to circumvent the fortresses of the Grey Mountains by leading a long column of his followers into the Empire via a narrow path known as the Crooked Corridor. Fortunately for the Empire, his plans came to naught as his scouts had failed to mention a small, but important detail… that their route passed in full view of the upper ramparts of Blackstone Tower, which was garrisoned at the time by Von Blucher's famous Reikland Sharpshooters. From this comes the triumphant expression, 'Like shooting Goblins in a gorge.'

The Black Mountains lie between the Grey Mountains and the Worlds Edge Mountains and divide the Empire from the wild southern lands of the Border Princes. The Black Mountains are possibly the least hospitable of all the Empire's borders, the skies wreathed in dark thunderheads as the towering crags climb towards the Vaults. The Black Mountains are notoriously riddled with crude Goblin tunnels and the entire mountain range is infested with countless deadly creatures that often venture down into the Empire to feed.

Forming the other main upland region within the Empire are the Middle Mountains, which lie in the northern reaches of the land. Middenheim, City of the White Wolf sits on the south-western tip of the Middle Mountains and beyond them is Ostland, northernmost province of the Empire. This massive range is surrounded by impenetrably dark forest and is shunned by all right-minded folk, as it is the domain of bandits and other undesirables. There are no large Dwarf delvings in these mountains, only inhospitable rocky uplands that no sane person would wish to explore. Deeper in the mountains the forbidding towers and high walls of Brass Keep, once an Imperial fastness, are now the refuge of the warriors of Chaos who have clawed themselves a foothold in the Empire. Graf Boris Todbringer of Middenheim has led armed expeditions to clear out these foes, but most of these forays into the mountains are doomed from the start and the Middle Mountains remain, for all intents and purposes, enemy territory.

The Mighty Rivers

Surrounded as it is by huge mountainous uplands, the Empire acts like a basin into which drain countless raging torrents. Beginning as crashing streams and spectacular waterfalls high in the mountains, these quickly converge to form spectacular, foaming rivers. By the time they reach the flat lands of the Empire they have become deep and substantial – the greatest waterways in all the Old World. These broad rivers are characteristic of the Empire, where travel by riverboat is often faster and more practical than travel through dangerous forests along primitive roads.

The people of the Empire tend to refer to the areas adjoining rivers by the names of the rivers themselves; Talabecland around the river Talabec, Reikland by the banks of the Reik, and so on. The River Sol is the southernmost of the Empire's rivers, cutting through what was once the province of Solland. Now part of Wissenland since Gorbad Ironclaw's invasion, there are some people of the Empire, mostly nobles from families that once lived in Solland, that refer to this region as Sudenland and refuse to acknowledge the rights of the Wissenland count.

The River Aver flows from the mountains above the the Dwarf fortress of Karak Varn just north of Black Fire Pass. Plunging over a series of immense waterfalls, these become two broad and startlingly blue rivers – the Aver Reach and the Blue Reach – that finally unite in the Halfling realm of the Moot. The River Aver continues westward past the provincial capital at Averheim and finally flows into the Reik at Nuln. The wide, fertile plains of Averland form prime grazing lands for horses and the steeds of this province are said to be the fastest horses of the Empire and hence in great demand by the quartermasters of the Knightly Orders.

The Stir flows from the western slopes of the Dwarf fortress of Karak Kadrin, quickly developing into a major river flowing within a deep, wooded valley that is said to be one of the most awe-inspiring vistas in the Empire. For virtually its entire length the Stir flows through the Great Forest and its breadth and few crossing points means that the river forms a defensive barrier and a border between Stirland and Talabecland. Since the Time of Three Emperors, these provinces have shared an uneasy peace at best and there have been many battles fought at important river crossings. In 2427, at the Battle of Leitziger Ford, the Elector Counts themselves fought a duel in the centre of the river. The combat ended with the Count of Stirland hacking the leg from his rival with a blow from his Runefang and the unfortunate Count of Talabecland being swept down the river where he had to be rescued by his Greatswords at battle's end. The severed leg was recovered by the soldiers of Stirland and, despite repeated requests by the Count of Talabecland's descendants to have the leg returned, the Counts of Stirland are quite fond of this trophy and seem determined to hang on to it.

The Talabec originates in the rapid streams between the Dwarf holds of Karak Kadrin and Karak Ungor. The river is named for the god Taal, Lord of Beasts. Two main forks flow westward, the Upper and Lower Talabec, converging in dark pine forests that have an evil reputation. In these hinterlands of the Empire there are bands of Orcs and Beastmen who descend from the mountains in search of prey and plunder. South of where it joins the Urskoy, the Talabec is broad and impossible to cross, becoming wider as it flows towards Talabheim. At Talabheim there is a ferry point and the banks of the river are fortified with cannon emplacements and a permanent garrison of the Elector Count's Greatswords to protect it.

The Upper Reik begins just south of Black Fire Pass and is joined by the Sol to the south of Nuln, continuing northwards until it converges with the Aver to form the Reik at Nuln. The Reik is the longest river in the Old World and the most important waterway in the Empire, making the Reikland its most prosperous province. It is a busy river, with fully laden merchant vessels travelling all the way from Marienburg to Nuln. This stretch of broad water carries more shipping than the rest of the rivers of the Empire put together, and it is the principal route for trade (and river banditry) in the Empire. Patrols of Shipswords and garrisons of River Wardens protect the Reik's river traffic, but while they are merciless with those they catch, it is impossible for them to prevent all piracy.

Altdorf is built upon an island formed of deposits of black soil carried from the Middle Mountains along the Talabec, and many shifting channels surround the city. These reunite into a single large body of water just north of Altdorf, and from here the river becomes broad and deep, with steep rocky islands thrusting up from the water, before reaching the sea at Marienburg.

TALABHEIM
THE EYE OF THE FOREST

Talabheim lies deep in the Great Forest and for this reason it is sometimes known as the Eye of the Forest, where, like the eye of a storm, all is calm amidst the surrounding danger. The city is built within a huge shallow crater, many miles across, whose outer edge forms a rocky rim and a natural wall. This wall has been built up and fortified with many tall gun towers and effectively marks the boundary of the town. The land inside is extensive and includes farmlands as well as the city itself. The River Talabec flows around the outside of the crater, and where it flows past the southern edge of the wall, there is a fortified settlement named Talagaad and a deep harbour. From the fortress of Talagaad, a narrow road climbs the ridge of the crater and enters the city via a tunnel carved through the rock of the rim wall. This tunnel is the only entrance to the city and a massive, fortified gateway at the end of the tunnel makes Talabheim one of the strongest cities in the Empire.

The Dark Forests

Gloomy, tangled forests cover much of the Empire and beneath their darkened boughs all manner of dreadful creatures and forgotten secrets are concealed. The forests are wild places, though there are many scattered settlements within the vast swathes of woodland. These are lonely pockets of civilisation, walled towns and villages where the gates are locked and barred every night and the surrounding forest regarded with dread. It is with reason that the people of the Empire fear what lurks in the forests, for the trees hide many foes: bandits, rampaging Orcs and mutated Chaos beasts. The deeper forests are virtually impenetrable. Few dare venture beyond sight of the treeline – and those that do are rarely seen again.

Connecting the villages and towns are perilous, rutted roads, with high-walled coaching inns scattered along their length. To be caught out in the forests at night is the terror of those who must brave the dangers of travelling through the forests, and the sight of a coaching inn through the darkness is a welcome one indeed. However, even such refuges are not without danger, and many tales are told of travellers who have discovered an inn completely empty, its inhabitants slaughtered by bandits or worse…

The Forest of Shadows is a brooding wood that lies north of the Middle Mountains and encompasses most of Ostland. The forest is thick with raiders, bandits and Chaos warbands – indeed, it is said that there are more brigands than trees. The necromancer Dieter Helsnicht was defeated at the Battle of Beekerhoven deep in the forest, but his body was never found, and tales persist that the Doomlord still haunts the forest.

West of the Middle Mountains lies the infamous Drakwald Forest, the region of the Empire that recalls the name of a lost province now overrun by Beastmen. The city of Middenheim stands atop its great crag of rock within the depths of the Drakwald and the Chaos beasts of the forest have ever been the scourge of the local people. When the inhabitants of the Empire shudder at the thought of monsters that bear the shape of Men fused with cattle, goats or vermin, they think of the Drakwald, for it is said to be home to the largest and most fearsome beasts imaginable. There is a standing bounty from the Count of Middenland for those that kill these beasts, bringing mercenaries from all over the world. Small wonder then that the people of the north are hardened to lives of battle, for theirs is a struggle against hunger, cold and the dangers of voracious forest creatures.

Ghostly mists thread the trees and the gloomy boughs echo to bestial howls and bellowing roars. The Knights of the White Wolf see these hunts as a good way to blood the Order's newer knights, and often sally deep into the Drakwald to cull the monstrous beasts in the name of Ulric. The road between Marienburg and Middenheim runs through this forest, though only those with a force of well-armed and resolute soldiers would dare travel this route for fear of ambush by the beasts of the forest. The Elector Counts of Nordland and Middenland have both attempted to establish fortified coaching inns along the road, but each attempt has ended in failure, with every single inn burned and all of their inhabitants slain and devoured.

Further south is the Great Forest, an ancient and colossal woodland that stretches from the Middle Mountains in the north to Nuln in the south, and from Altdorf in the west to the borders of Kislev in the east. Together with the other mighty forest lands of the Empire it forms an unimaginably vast heartland of darkened, twisted trees that dominates the central area of the Empire. A goodly portion of the Empire's population dwell within the bounds of the Great Forest. As a result, countless acres of it have been cleared to allow for cultivation, or to provide logs for the hillside forts which are the main defence against the terrible creatures that lurk in the forest's depths. Roving bands of Flagellants are a common – if not exactly welcome – sight in the Great Forest, bloodied processions of whipping, screaming madmen marching from town to town and spreading their apocalyptic dogma to all they encounter.

The Reikwald Forest lies to the south of Altdorf between the River Reik and the Grey Mountains. It is a favourite haunt of those who have been outcast from the Empire, where fugitives from justice take to an existence of brigandry. Though but a few leagues from the Empire's centre of power, there is scant resolve to clear the forest, as it provides a ready source of expendable militia regiments to the Emperor's banner when he marches to war. Many bandits of this region are content to turn a coin fighting as mercenaries and, though they are neither as reliable or as well trained as state troops, the Emperor knows that while they fight in his army they are not robbing his lands!

MARIENBURG
CITYPORT OF MERCHANTS

At the mouth of the River Reik stands Marienburg, the world's marketplace – the largest, richest, most corrupt and most dangerous cityport in the Old World. Here, everything is for sale, and nothing is without a price. Marienburg is often known as the City of Gold, which alone conveys a good idea of the wealth of this sprawling, cosmopolitan city. Nowhere else can goods from as far away as the Elven kingdoms of Ulthuan or distant Cathay be found so readily. Once a city of the Empire, the city's Burgomeisters colluded with Emperor Dieter IV to secure their independence in return for a massive donation of gold to the Imperial coffers. When this scandalous affair came to light, Dieter was quickly deposed and Wilhelm III of Altdorf, Prince of the Reikland, became the new Emperor. Numerous attempts over the past decades to restore Marienburg to the Empire have all failed, and the city remains so fiercely independent that the Count of Nordland (nominally the ruler of Marienburg) is forbidden to return under pain of an excruciatingly hideous death.

THE AGE OF KARL FRANZ

When Karl Franz, Prince of Altdorf and Count of Reikland was elected to the imperial Throne in 2502, the Empire was enjoying a period of relative peace and stability. However, the new Emperor was well aware that such a situation would not last and that it would take all of his skills as a commander and a statesman to protect the Empire and its people for generations to come.

The General

Wishing to establish his reign as one of military strength and to send a message to those outside his borders that he was not a man to be taken lightly, the Emperor decided a show of force would ratify his position as Emperor.

Since the Great War Against Chaos, the numbers of Beastmen and Chaos worshippers had been growing steadily once more. Karl Franz's advisors told him that in the far north, the winds of magic were blowing strongly again. It might not be for years, even decades, but at some time, the marauders would come again in force, pushed south by the expansion of the Chaos Wastes. Norse raiders, growing bolder in recent years, had reaped a bloody toll on the people dwelling on the coast of the Sea of Claws, slaughtering entire towns and carrying off their livestock and womenfolk. In response, Karl Franz's first act was to march northwards at the head of a mighty host to reinforce the army of Theoderic Gausser, Elector Count of Nordland. Nordland's armies could not know where the Norse would strike in time to defend their people, but the Emperor had brought with him some of the most powerful wizards of the Celestial College, whose members are gifted with the ability to read the future in the heavens.

The next time the Norse raiders attacked, they were met with fusillades of fire from concealed handgunners and crossbowmen and their ships sunk by unerringly accurate cannon fire. Hundreds of Norse died without a fight as their heavy hauberks dragged them to the bottom of the sea and those that survived to reach the shore were met by disciplined ranks of swordsmen, spearmen and halberdiers marching onto the beach. The berserk Norsemen were slaughtered without quarter, and the Emperor himself led the charge against the final Norse shieldwall.

As the years passed, the Empire continued to grow in power and influence, with the Emperor engaging in many great public works to improve the lot of his people. Through Kurt Helborg, the Emperor enacted his will, despatching the Master of the Reiksguard to lead his armies in battle against numerous foes; the Ogre reavers of Gutlord Breaskus, the Orcs of the Blighted Towers and a rumoured infestation of the foul ratmen in the Howling Hills – the site of Emperor Mandred's famous victory against the underfolk.

The Emperor himself once again marched to war in 2519 at the request of Marius Leitdorf, the Elector Count of Averland. Dwarf Rangers had brought word of a massive horde of greenskins marching westwards through the Worlds Edge Mountains, and the ill-trained and poorly led provincial army of Averland would not be able to hold them back. With the might of the Reikland behind him, Karl Franz stemmed the tide of Orcs and left garrisons to aid the Averlanders in maintaining their borders.

Despite receiving the Emperor's aid, the Mad Count of Averland continued to cause problems for Karl Franz – challenging the other Counts, leading nonsensical military campaigns after imaginary foes and generally upsetting his neighbours. After Leitdorf's ruthless suppression of the infamous Halfling Rebellion of 2502, Karl Franz despatched the dour Emperor's Champion, Ludwig Schwarzhelm, to hold robust negotiations with the eccentric Elector Count. The cheerless Schwarzhelm's orders were simple – he was to ensure that Leitdorf's notoriously unpredictable behaviour did not imperil the Empire any further.

ELECTOR COUNTS
AND OTHER EMPIRE ELECTORS

Averland	Disputed
Hochland	Aldebrand Ludenhof
Middenland	Graf Boris Todbringer
Nordland	Theoderic Gausser
Ostland	Valmir von Raukov
Ostermark	Wolfram Hertwig
Reikland	Emperor Karl Franz
Stirland	Graf Alberich Haupt-Anderssen
Talabecland	Helmut Feuerbach (missing)
Wissenland	Emmanuelle von Liebwitz
Solland	Eldred (last Count*)
Drakwald	Konrad Aldrech (last Count*)
The Moot	Hisme Stoutheart
	Grand Theogonist Volkmar
	Arch Lector Kaslain
	Arch Lector Aglim
	Ar Ulric Emil Valgeir

*The Provinces of Solland and Drakwald no longer exist and the named Counts are the last of that particular Province.

With some unsubtle guidance from Karl Franz through Schwarzhelm, Marius Leitdorf appointed new advisors to curb the worst of his excesses. Having been returned to the fold of the Emperor's trusted allies, Leitdorf sent word to Karl Franz when Orcs once again invaded along Black Fire Pass. Karl Franz responded in person and arrived with his army to face the Orc and Goblin horde. It was with geniune regret that the Emperor witnessed the death of Leitdorf at the hands of the Orc Cheiftain. Karl Franz smashed apart the creature's skull with Ghal Maraz, and later claimed this bloody retribution had been divinely inspired by the spirit of Sigmar.

The Statesman

The Empire continued to flourish under the rulership of Karl Franz, though there were ever dangers to face and enemies to fight. When hostilities erupted between Graf Alberich Haupt-Anderssen of Stirland and Helmut Feuerbach of Talabecland, ancestral enemies since the Time of Three Emperors, the other Counts waited expectantly to see which side Karl Franz would back. The Emperor travelled to Talabheim in an attempt to negotiate peace between the two hostile provinces.

The Emperor's skill in debate was put to the ultimate test in resolving the dispute, as was his patience, but in the end both Elector Counts acceded to Karl Franz's wisdom and a potentially bitter civil war was ended before it began. Many other potential conflicts have been resolved through Karl Franz attending such negotiations, not least in part because he is always flanked by the unsmiling figure of Ludwig Schwarzhelm. The sight of the Emperor's personal champion with the Sword of Justice unsheathed has usually been enough to make most Elector Counts settle their differences without recourse to war.

On another memorable occasion, the aggressive Count of Nordland's territorial ambitions against the neighbouring province of Hochland were averted when the Emperor requested the Supreme Patriarch of the Colleges of Magic, Balthasar Gelt, to intervene. Advised by Karl Franz, Gelt travelled to Castle Salzenmund, seat of Theoderic Gausser, Elector Count of Nordland. Though ostensibly there as the Emperor's ambassador, Gelt secretly transmuted the gold earmarked for the Count's armies and mercenaries into worthless bars of lead. The hired swords refused to fight without payment and the looming threat of civil war was averted. As soon as he

discovered what had happened, the enraged Elector Count drew his Runefang and swore he would have Gelt's head, but his murderous ambitions were thwarted, as the Supreme Patriarch had wisely left Nordland in a hurry on the back of his Pegasus.

The Champion of Sigmar

As the Emperor's counsellors and court had feared, the threat of Chaos was to rise again during Karl Franz's reign. As autumn turned to winter in 2521 famine stalked the land after the worst harvest in living memory. The people of the Empire cried aloud to the gods to deliver them from these evil times as ill portents were seen throughout the land and superstitious fear spread like never before. A twin-tailed comet lit up the skies over the Empire and doomsayers and demagogues claimed that this was surely a sign of the End Times. Rumours abounded of Archaon the Everchosen, a mighty warlord who was gathering an army such as had not been seen in the northern wastes since the Great War Against Chaos. Karl Franz knew that action must be taken to save his

land from impending doom. In secret, he sent word to the Elves of Ulthuan and asked their Phoenix King if he would send his armies to fight alongside Karl Franz just as they had done for Magnus the Pious. Envoys also travelled to the High King of the Dwarfs.

While Karl Franz made his diplomatic moves, an army led by the Grand Theogonist, Volkmar the Grim, was slaughtered in the frozen wastes of the Troll Country and the fiery High Priest of the Cult of Sigmar was taken by the Daemon, Be'lakor. In the wake of this defeat, people flocked to the temples and shrines of Sigmar, praying for deliverance from Archaon's evil as he led his host southwards. With invasion imminent, Karl Franz summoned the rulers of the Old World to the Conclave of Light in Altdorf, and the nations of Men, and even the Dwarfs and Elves, came together in common cause to fight the forces of Chaos.

The land of Kislev fell to the might of Archaon and the Ostermark and Ostland were ravaged by the hordes of Chaos. In the midst of this despair, the renegade Warrior Priest, Luthor Huss, presented a young man named Valten to Karl Franz and proclaimed him Sigmar reborn. Huss had rallied a great deal of support and thus the Emperor could not simply dismiss his grand claims. Karl Franz presented Valten with Ghal Maraz and dubbed him the Champion of Sigmar – though prudently retained rulership of the Empire, and command of its armies for himself. The Emperor bade Kurt Helborg muster the Counts and their forces, and ordered Ludwig Schwarzhelm to unfurl the Imperial Banner.

The Victorious Leader

Middenheim echoed to the raucous clamour of battle as the brave defenders of the Empire fought the innumerable hordes of Archon's warriors. The armies of the northern provinces refused to buckle and held their foes at bay until the Emperor and his allies came to their aid. Karl Franz waged a masterful campaign against the many foes arrayed against the Empire. At the height of the battle, Archaon and Valten fought at the base of the Ulricsberg, and though Archaon was vanquished, Valten was grievously wounded. Kurt Helborg led the Reiksguard Knights in a final charge and the forces of Chaos were scattered. The war was over, but a terrible tragedy was yet to come to light. The body of Valten was found, slain by an assassin's blade. Weeping, Luthor Huss carried the Hammer of Sigmar back to the Emperor. The Emperor knew that his people needed hope in the aftermath of war. When Valten's body mysteriously disappeared, Karl Franz spoke to Huss:

"You shall go forth among the people and say that Sigmar has left us, as he did so many centuries ago. Give them hope in these dark times. Do not betray their faith. Tell them that he has left his hammer to me, as a sign of his trust, and tell them that you are still his prophet and shall look for his return again when we most need him."

THE COLLEGES OF MAGIC

From the time of Sigmar, sorcery in all of its forms was the greatest crime in the Empire and those with magical powers were ruthlessly hunted down. However, during the time of the Great War Against Chaos, the Elven Mage Teclis fought side-by-side with the armies of Magnus the Pious. To better combat the forces of Chaos, Teclis assembled the low sorcerers of the Empire and taught them rudimentary spells of fire and lightning bolts. These new Battle Wizards proved an invaluable, if not entirely trusted, addition to Magnus' armies.

Upon his ascension to the throne, Magnus asked Teclis to pass on his magical lore to the Men of the Empire and, despite the misgivings of his companions, the great Mage agreed. Teclis realised that the magical powers of men needed to be controlled or they would threaten the future of the world, and he gathered the most powerful of the Human Wizards and established the Colleges of Magic in Altdorf. Teclis taught that all magic was derived from Chaos, but that it could be controlled and purified by a trained practitioner. Men learned how magic blew from the northern realms of Chaos in the form of eight sorcerous winds, each of which represented a unique Lore of Magic. For this reason the sign of all magic is the symbol of Chaos itself – the

eight-pointed star – and for each lore Teclis founded a separate school of magic and taught its first masters. The minds of Men were inadequate to master all eight Winds of Magic, but with care and study a Wizard could master the power of a single Lore.

Thus today there are eight Colleges, each of which forms the nexus of one of the Orders of Magic in the Empire. Each has its own Masters, and the sorcery of each is different and distinct from the others, yet all are aspects of that great and potent source of magic that is Chaos.

The Light Order

The Wizards of the Light Order are sometimes known as White Wizards or Hierophants as their study is knowledge. For this reason they are also called the Order of the Wise and rulers from all over the Old World seek their counsel. The Lore of Light lies under the province of the First Lore of Magic, which is called the Wind of Hysh and whose symbol is the Serpent of Light. This Lore is said to be the most difficult to master and its spells are especially elaborate and ritualistic. The magic of the Order is most renowned for its powers of healing and protection, yet a Light Wizard can conjure blazing lights that can blind and burn.

Like many of the magical colleges, the College of Light goes largely unseen, as it exists within a magical space, parallel to but separate from the mundane world. To those who chance upon its whereabouts, the building appears as a gigantic pyramid whose translucent walls shimmer with power and the light of thousands of candles. It is an awesome sight indeed and one that few of Altdorf's inhabitants would imagine lies within their city. Deep in the darkest dungeons of the College, protected by many twisting tunnels, traps, and magical fields, lies the greatest magical treasure vault in the Old World. Created by Teclis after the Great War Against Chaos, it serves as a repository and prison for many of the evil artefacts and luminous beings of power captured during that conflict. It is the sacred duty of the Guardians of the Light, an arcane society to which only the most powerful Wizards of the Order belong, to keep these powerful evils safely locked away from the world.

The Golden Order

The Wizards of the Golden Order study the Lore of Metal or Alchemy that flows upon the Wind of Chamon. Their symbol is a soaring eagle and the Wizards of the Golden Order are the most accomplished alchemists of all Humans in the Old World. They practise the transmutation of metals as well as spells of forging and runic inscription. Though inferior in the latter regard to Dwarf Runesmiths, they are much less affected by the maddening power that gold has over Dwarfs and so have the mastery of many spells that no Runesmith would dare attempt. Though much of the Gold Order's magic is of an alchemical nature, its Wizards are able to conjure molten metals that scorch and consume and their magic can corrode and weaken iron in the blink of an eye.

The buildings of the Golden Order are neither rich nor ostentatious, but are more akin to great forges with many furnaces and tall chimneys that belch glowing, multi-coloured smoke into the air. This College lies not near the centre of the city (much to the relief of the citizens of Altdorf) but upon its edge by the River Reik. The river cools the forges and it is a common sight to see the waters running with fantastical colours in the wake of some mysterious experiment. The Golden College is not hidden from view like some magical colleges, but few dare approach it for fear of the evil vapours and crackling magical energies that surround it.

The Jade Order

The Wizards of the Jade Order study the Lore of Life that springs from the Wind of Ghyran. The symbol of the Third Order is the Coil of Life and Jade Wizards often go barefoot to better feel the Wind of Ghyran upon their feet. Jade Wizards love life and living things, for their studies teach them of the harmony of nature and the balance between the land and the creatures that dwell upon it. Jade Wizards roam the forests and wild places of the Empire where the power of magic flows through the world most freely. With a gesture they can conjure forests, summon mighty storms from a cloudless sky or cause the very rocks of the earth to fly into the air. As in nature, so too does a Jade Wizard's powers wax and wane with the seasons, being youthful and vigorous in spring, most powerful in the summer, waning over the autumn and becoming weakest in the depths of winter.

There are many hidden groves of ancient stone circles scattered throughout the Empire where the Jade Order conducts its rituals and keeps many of its most secret treasures. These often lie at the confluence of three streams, for such places are strong with magic. Within Altdorf itself, the College takes the form of a plain and unimposing enclosure to the outside world, yet within is a wondrous arbor of beautiful trees whose boughs form the beams and pillars of numerous mighty halls. Glittering pools and streams flow amongst the glades of this hidden world and at its centre is a wondrous silver lake where the power of Ghyran collects and whose enchanted waters are said to be able to cure all maladies.

The Celestial Order

The Wizards of the Celestial Order study the Lore of the Heavens that comes from the Wind of Azyr. The symbol of this Order is the Comet of Power and Celestial Wizards spend most of their time gazing into the night skies and plotting the movements of astral bodies on bafflingly complex trans-chronological charts. They are experts in the manufacture of astrolabes and telescopes, devices by which the paths of the future can be glimpsed, and thus the advice of the Celestial Order is valued above that of all others in times of war or hardship. Though most often sought out as seers to foretell of danger and disaster, they are equally respected for the awesome powers that lie at their disposal. Their spells are able to call lightning from the skies or draw hunks of star-borne rock from beyond the heavens to smite their enemies.

The sixteen glittering towers of the Celestial College are the tallest buildings in Altdorf, overlooking the Temple of Sigmar and rising far above the Emperor's Palace. None but those with magical sight would know of this, for cunning spells of concealment shield the buildings of the Celestial College from the curiosity of passers-by. A shimmering dome of magical glass sits atop each tower, enchanted to allow the Celestial Wizards to focus on specific aspects of the night sky, and from these observatories the Wizards of the Celestial Order plot the movements of the heavens. Information gathered from the towers is fed into a magical astrolabe at the heart of the College that spins on the head of a silver needle and from which the Celestial Wizards read the myriad potential futures.

WITCH HUNTERS

The practice of magic beyond the strictures of the Colleges of Magic in Altdorf is utterly forbidden and is a crime punishable by the most painful death. Those that dare to employ fell sorcery are branded malevolent witches and it is the duty of the much-feared witch hunters to hunt down and destroy such nefarious villains. This work is incredibly dangerous and is undertaken by only the boldest of souls who hold the faith of Sigmar close to their hearts, for rogue sorcerers and witches are powerful enemies who gather all manner of vile creatures of Chaos to them. Though given to a terse and brooding manner, witch hunters are seldom solitary individuals. Indeed, witch hunters often recruit warbands of warriors, priests and Wizards to accompany them in their travails, for the prey of a witch hunter is fought not only in the land of the physical, but also in the realms of the spiritual and magical.

THE HALL OF DUELS

The master of the Colleges of Magic is known as the Supreme Patriarch and his word is law in all matters magical throughout the Empire. The Winds of Magic blow strongest for the Supreme Patriarch's Order and fellow Wizards of that order find their powers greatly enhanced during his reign. Every eight years, a Wizard who has proved himself worthy may challenge the current Supreme Patriarch to a magical combat held in the Hall of Duels. This octagonal chamber contains the Staff of Volans at its centre and the Wizard who is able to grasp this ancient artefact will become the new Supreme Patriarch of the Colleges of Magic.

As soon as the duel commences, mighty spells of great power and cunning are unleashed in a magical conflict that can only be safely contained by the combined powers of a dozen or more Master Wizards. Tradition demands that the duel is not fought to the death, though on more than one occasion the magical feedback has left little of the loser to be buried, and even the victor is likely to nurse a scar or two as a reminder. More worrisome, but fortunately much rarer, are those occasions when there is a cataclysmic failure of the magical wards about the duel and a roiling cloud of uncontrolled magic escapes, wreaking havoc as it courses through the streets of Altdorf.

The Grey Order

The Wizards of the Grey Order study the Lore of Shadow that is known as the Wind of Ulgu. This secretive Lore of Magic is at its strongest in the dank, threatening fogs and mists that bring a chill to the air and hide everything in a cloak of darkness. The symbol of the Order is the Sword of Judgement and each Wizard usually carries a sword beneath his robes. Of all the Orders of Wizards they are the least trusted or liked by common folk who believe them to be sinister and scheming. For this reason they are sometimes called Trickster Wizards, though they call themselves the Grey Guardians.

Grey Wizards are wanderers by nature, whose journeys always seem to imply some great or sinister purpose. Yet they do not talk easily of their deeds, or of other matters much, for they are aware of the distrust of their fellow Men and prefer to remain inconspicuous. Their powers, though considerable, do not lend themselves well to the favour of ordinary folk, being bound up in spells of concealment and illusion by a number of baleful and unseen ways.

The Grey College itself is a worn and shabby building, in Altdorf's poorest and most disreputable district. Even the city watch shun this area and no honest citizen would ordinarily risk entering such a den of rogues. Though the building appears unremarkable, Grey Wizards come and go by a multitude of secret entrances and a warren of magical tunnels extending beneath the building – where they emerge is a mystery known only to the Order's Wizards.

The Amethyst Order

The Wizards of the Amethyst Order study the Lore of Death that is carried on the Wind of Shyish and blows strongly in places where the stench of death lies most heavily. Its energies are drawn to the dying and the doom that follows the end of mortality. It blows over battlefields and mortuaries, it clings around charnel pits and Gardens of Morr, and falls over the gibbet and gallows like a shadow. Amethyst Wizards are swathed in robes decorated with the scythe, the hourglass and the thorned rose, images that all folk of the Empire recognise as symbols of the grave. They have mastery over spirits, and it is said that they can steal souls or suck the life from the living, leaving naught but a withered husk. They can summon carrion winds of death that rot flesh and envelop their foes in a black shroud of unending, suicidal despair. Such abilities are as nothing compared to the nightmarish sorceries of necromancy, yet their association with death forever taints Amethyst Wizards in the eyes of their fellow Men.

The College building of the Amethyst Order is dark and sepulchral, shuttered against the light and only dimly illuminated even in the dead of night. Within its silent halls the dust lies thick where it is dragged by the Winds of Shyish from all the ages, bringing with it the stench of eternal decay. Though the citizens of Altdorf are fully aware of this building, none dare approach it for fear of damning their immortal soul forever. Its crooked towers are the abode of bats and carrion birds, and its cellars crawl with all manner of verminous creatures.

The Amethyst College overlooks the infamous haunted Cemetery of Old Altdorf, where thousands were interred in mass graves after the ravages of the Red Plague. The cemetary itself is associated with all manner of foul rumour, and the Amethyst Order's proximity to it is taken by many as proof of unholy practices by the secretive Wizards. True evidence of such deeds has yet to come to light, but still the good citizens of Altdorf give both the cemetary and College a wide berth, leaving the Order to their secrets.

The Bright Order

The Lore of Fire, or Pyromancy, sears upon the Wind of Aqshy and is the province of the Wizards of the Bright Order. The Key of Secrets is their symbol, representing the unlocking of hidden knowledge, and Wizards of the Order often carry bronze keys as signs of their authority. Bright Wizards are ruddy of skin and are frequently adorned with tattoos that writhe and change form to weave spells of fire. The energies of Aqshy are powerful where there is fire, and by means of their powers, Bright Wizards control smoke and flame.

When it comes to battle, Bright Wizards are held above all others for theirs is one of the most spectacular and destructive Lores of Magic. A Bright Wizard can wield flame like a sword, hurl fireballs and raise searing walls of fire to burn his enemies. Such powers are incredibly destructive, and few ordinary folk would seek the assistance of a Bright Wizard, for wherever their powers are employed, ruin and devastation is sure to follow.

Spectacular, fire-topped towers that blaze with magical light form the College of the Bright Wizards, though its fiery brilliance lies concealed behind a barrier of powerful illusion. To those without magical sight, the College's buildings appear as dark and splintered ruins in a wasteland of ashen destruction, but in the heat of summer they sometimes appear as a shimmering mirage, floating above the city like a veil of glittering rubies. At the heart of the Bright College's towers is a gigantic beacon that burns both day and night, and casts an eerie red glow over the entire College. Within its fiery depths are the conjurations of the Bright Order conceived.

The Amber Order

The Wizards of the Amber Order are devotees of the Lore of Beasts, which is heard as the cry of an eagle upon the Wind of Ghur. The Wizards of this Order can be recognised by their savage appearance and primitive talismans. Their symbol is the Arrow, which is the sign of the hunter, and they are known as Shamans by some and Brown Wizards by others. Amber Wizards are solitary individuals, preferring the company of wild beasts to their fellow Men, and they avoid settlements unless they have some need that draws them from the mountains or forests.

Their magic is merciless and inhuman, caring little for the ways of Mankind and recognising the savage heart that lies under the veneer of civilisation that adorns every Human soul. The power of the Amber Wizards resides most strongly in the minds of wild animals and to learn the ways of the Amber Order is to open one's mind to the raw and savage power of the wild. Empire folklore is rife with tales of Wizards with the power to become wild creatures or far-travelling birds. Amber Wizards can commune with animals of all kinds and have the ability to assume the strength of the greatest beasts or induce states of animal terror in others.

Of all the Orders of Wizardry, the Amber College is the only one without buildings in Altdorf. Its masters inhabit the caves high in the Amber Hills beyond the city, which take their name from the order. These refuges are not easily found and visitors are not welcomed. Other lairs are said to exist throughout the Empire in the depths of forests and high on mountaintops, but monstrous bears or other powerful wild beasts guard these solitary caves and it is a brave individual who dares disturb an Amber Wizard.

A TIMELINE OF THE EMPIRE

Imperial Calendar

-500   Rise of Humanity in the Old World. Numerous warlords and petty kings war amongst themselves to establish realms in the Old World. Goblins, Beastmen and other vile creatures prey upon these scattered tribes.

-50   Artur, chief of Teutogens, discovers the Fauschlag rock (later known as the Ulricsberg), and enlists the aid of the Dwarfs to build a fortress that will be known as Middenheim.

-30   Sigmar is born, son of the chief of the Unberogen tribe.

-15   A Dwarf trading convoy from Karaz-a-Karak is ambushed on its way to the Grey Mountains and King Kurgan Ironbeard is captured by Orcs. He is rescued by Sigmar and, in gratitude, Kurgan gifts Sigmar the rune hammer Ghal Maraz.

-8   Upon the death of his father, Sigmar becomes chief of the Unberogen tribe.

-1   The Battle of Black Fire Pass. A massive horde of Orcs and Goblins are driven from lands west of the Worlds Edge Mountains.

1   Sigmar crowned Emperor at Reikdorf by the High Priest of Ulric. Alaric the Mad begins the creation of the Runefangs.

50   After a half century of building and prosperity in the newly proclaimed Empire, Sigmar vanishes into the east, never to be seen again. The system of Elector Counts is established whereby the provincial leaders elect one of their number to be Emperor.

63   Wulcan, High Priest of Ulric, has a vision of Ulric and builds a temple in Middenheim.

73   The rapidly spreading Cult of Sigmar, patron deity of the Empire, receives its first High Priest (later to be known as the Grand Theogonist), Johann Helsturm.

c100   Emperor Hedrich is presented with the Runefangs by Alaric the Mad and he passes them to the Elector Counts.

100 to 500   The Cult of Sigmar is now widespread, leading to conflict with the Cult of Ulric.

501   Marienburg is absorbed by the Empire during the reign of Emperor Sigismund II.

1000   Birth of the Old World nations and fragmentation of the Empire due to plague and civil disorder. To the dismay of the Elector Counts, Ludwig the Fat issues a royal charter to the Halflings of the Moot, granting them administrative autonomy and an Imperial vote.

1053 to 1115   Reign of Boris Goldgather. Corruption is rife.

1111 to 1115   Skaven unleash the Black Plague in the Empire. Nine-tenths of the Empire's population is wiped out in the next four years as massive Skaven incursions loot and raze towns and villages, systematically enslaving the surviving settlements in the Empire.

1115   The death of Boris Goldgather from the Black Plague. Despite the misery of the Empire, celebrations are held all across the land.

1122   Count Mandred rallies support from the Elector Counts and leads a crusade against the Skaven. They are driven out in 1124 at the Battle of the Howling Hills and Mandred, now known as the Ratslayer, is elected Emperor.

1152   Assassination of Emperor Mandred by the Skaven. The Elector Counts cannot agree upon a successor and the Empire divides into self-governing provinces.

1359   After years of deliberation, the Elector Counts name Grand Duke of Stirland the new Emperor and he is crowned in Nuln.

1360   Ottilia of Talabecland declares herself Empress, and over the next few hundred years there are two Emperors: the elected Emperor and the reigning Count of Talabecland.

c1435   Sultan Jaffar, a powerful Arabyan sorcerer, welds together a coalition of several desert tribes and expands his city state to a small empire. Legend speaks of him summoning Daemons and conversing with spirits.

c1450   The Crusades against Araby. Many Empire Knightly Orders fight during the Crusades, freeing Estalia and taking the war to Araby itself. Jaffar's empire is destroyed.

1547 The Count of Middenheim proclaims himself Emperor. There are now three Emperors. None of them commands much loyalty amongst the other provinces and each effectively rules an independent state.

1550 Middenland becomes a separate province.

1604 The first steps are taken to establish democratic government in Marienburg.

1707 The Orc warlord Gorbad Ironclaw invades the Empire through Black Fire Pass. Nuln is sacked and the Moot devastated. Solland is overrun and its Elector Count slain – after this, Solland ceases to exist as a separate land. The Solland Runefang is captured by Orcs. Gorbad advances north and a large Imperial army under the Count of Wissenland is defeated at the Battle of Grunberg just south of Altdorf. The city is besieged and Emperor Sigismund (the elected Emperor at this time) is killed by a Wyvern, but Altdorf holds out.

1797 Vlad von Carstein becomes the first of the Vampire Counts of Sylvania. Over the next two centuries the remaining noble families are infected with the curse of Vampirism.

1979 Magritta of Marienburg is elected Empress, but the Grand Theogonist refuses to acknowledge her appointment and the Imperial system is effectively ended. Mercantile Burgomeisters of the cities grow in power.

2000 Mordheim is destroyed by a comet.

2001 Finubar of the High Elves lands at Bretonnian port of L'Anguille. He travels extensively and opens relations with the Empire, Bretonnia and even the Dwarfs.

2010 Wars of the Vampire Counts begin with the devastation of Ostermark by Vlad von Carstein. Undead armies rampage between Stirland and the northern border.

2025 Vlad von Carstein is slain by Grand Master Kruger of the Knights of the White Wolf. A year later, Kruger's body is found at the base of the Ulricsberg, drained of blood.

2051 Vlad von Carstein returns, but is slain at the Siege of Altdorf. The Vampire Counts fight amongst themselves and their undead army splinters into feuding forces.

2121 Konrad von Carstein emerges as the most powerful Vampire Count. He leads his forces against the Empire, but a combined Empire and Dwarf army finally destroys him at the Battle of Grim Moor in 2121.

2132 to 2145 Mannfred von Carstein, the last and most cunning of the Vampire Counts, launches an attack against the Empire while it is locked in a vicious civil war. His army reaches and almost destroys Altdorf, but is defeated and driven back. Determined to end the threat of the Vampire Counts forever, the armies of the Elector Counts finally bring him to bay at Hel Fenn, where his Undead army is destroyed.

2302 The Great War Against Chaos begins as the forces of Chaos march south across the Lynsk and lay siege to Praag. The city falls in the winter of 2302/2303.

2303 to 2304 Magnus the Pious of Nuln defeats the Chaos armies at the gates of Kislev and is elected Emperor. Rebuilding of the Empire. Magnus establishes his court at Nuln. Teclis of the High Elves founds the Colleges of Magic in Altdorf.

2369 On Magnus' death, the Imperial crown passes, not to his brother, Gunthar von Bildhofen (who antagonised the Grand Theogonist), but to Count Leopold of Stirland.

2420 to 2424 The Goblin warlord Grom leads a coalition of Orc and Goblin tribes into the Worlds Edge Mountains. After defeating the Dwarfs at the Battle of Iron Gate, Grom moves into the Empire. Much of the north and east is devastated and Nuln is sacked. Grom leads his armies to the sea where he builds a huge fleet and sails into the west, never to be seen again in the Old World.

2429 Marienburg secedes from the Empire after the Burgomeisters collude with Emperor Dieter IV to secure their independence in return for vast amounts of Marienburger gold. Dieter is deposed after the ensuing scandal. The Imperial crown passes to Wilhelm III, Prince of Altdorf and Count of Reikland, remaining with his family to the present day.

2502 Accession of Karl Franz, the reigning Emperor.

2521 to 2522 United under Archaon, Lord of the End Times, marauders from the Chaos Wastes pour south in a massive invasion known as the Storm of Chaos. The armies of the Old World (and beyond) stand together against Archaon, and the forces of Chaos are driven back into the Middle Mountains.

FORCES OF THE EMPIRE

This section of the book details the forces of an Empire army. It provides the rules necessary to use all of the elements of the army in your games of Warhammer. Every character and regiment is described, including some of the Empire's greatest heroes, such as the Emperor Karl Franz, the Grand Marshal of the Reiksguard, Kurt Helborg, and Volkmar, Grand Theogonist of the Cult of Sigmar. Any special rules that apply to a particular model are given here, including the rules for Empire state troops and their detachments. Also included in this section are details of the crazed inventions of the Engineers, as well as the powerful magical artefacts carried by the heroes of the Empire.

COMMANDERS OF THE EMPIRE

To command an army requires the courage to send soldiers to what may be their deaths without doubt or hesitation. The armies of the Empire are led by warriors who have been trained to direct their forces as effortlessly as a swordsman wields a blade.

Of course, these commanders can differ in skill and bravery, with some, like the ferocious Elector Count of Middenheim, Boris Todbringer, embodying the unwavering valour of Sigmar's folk. Others are effete fops, yet still command men in battle thanks to their ancestral titles.

The castles of these generals are hung with banners from ancient times that were once borne aloft by their illustrious forefathers. Particularly wealthy nobles may even own a banner woven with potent enchantments, and these banners are proudly carried into battle.

The Empire is a dangerous land, with marauding Beastmen, Orc tribes or even rival nobles pillaging its towns and slaughtering its people. The Elector Counts must fight such foes, though in practice it is unfeasible for them to command every force that must be despatched. Often command is delegated to a trusted soldier considered to be an honourable leader of Men, and this officer will lead the province's forces in battle. Of course there are always exceptions, and some of the more bellicose counts (such as Valmir von Raukov of Ostland) have an unhealthy love for the clash of swords or the thunder of cannon and take to the field of battle whenever they can.

Many of the Men appointed by the Elector Count will also be nobles of the Empire, such as Aldebrand Ludenhof of Hochland, educated in martial pursuits from an early age – hunting Beastmen in the forests, falconry and swordsmanship. Others have risen through the ranks, having first stood in the battle line with a bloody halberd in their hands. These officers vary greatly in rank, depending on the size of the force they lead, and can be known as captains, marshals, generals or simply commanders. Regardless of their station, they will be tried and tested veterans of many years who understand the craft of soldiering better than anyone, having spent most of their lives fighting in defence of their homeland.

	M	WS	BS	S	T	W	I	A	Ld
General	4	5	5	4	4	3	5	3	9
Captain	4	5	5	4	4	2	5	3	8

THE IMPERIAL ZOO

The Imperial Zoo was founded in Altdorf by the hated Emperor Dieter IV and is home to some of the most dangerous monsters of the Old World. All manner of grotesque monstrosities (such as the Abomination of Stirland and the Spawn of Hochland) are held captive here and thus it is one of the most popular attractions in the city. In addition to being one of the wonders of the Old World, the zoo also has a practical function, stabling the Emperor's war steeds – Warhorses, Griffons, Pegasus and the mighty Imperial Dragon.

Warhorse

A Warhorse is a steed that has been trained to carry its rider into the chaos of battle without fear and to lash out with its iron-shod hooves. The most prized Empire Warhorses are those reared in Averland, for they are renowned for their strength and speed.

Griffon

Griffons are wild creatures that hunt from the tallest crags of the Worlds Edge Mountains, soaring on huge, feathered wings. A Griffon's head and forequarters resemble those of a powerful eagle, its hooked beak and clawed forelegs easily able to tear through plate armour. Behind its wings a Griffon's body is furred and massively powerful, its hindquarters those of a mighty lion. Their pelts can vary enormously in appearance, some with golden fur like that of a great mountain cat, while others are striped or spotted like the pelisses worn by the heroic Knights Panther.

Imperial Pegasus

A Pegasus is a winged beast that resembles the mightiest of horses, with a hide the colour of virgin snow and an intelligence beyond that of any other steed. Their nests are found high in the Grey Mountains, and if a Pegasus is ever to accept a rider, it must be captured while still a foal. It takes many years of patient training to gain the trust of a Pegasus, but once that trust is established, they are loyal mounts that will obey their master's every command.

The Imperial Dragon

Dragons are monstrous beasts with great, sweeping wings that bear them and their rider effortlessly through the sky. Huge and terrifying, they can rend their foes with powerful talons and swallow a Man whole in their fanged jaws. Only one Dragon is kept in the Imperial zoo, raised from an egg said to have been taken from the deepest cave in the Black Mountains. Only the Emperor Karl Franz himself dares to ride this mighty Dragon for only he has the strength of will to dominate its cold, aloof mind.

	M	WS	BS	S	T	W	I	A	Ld
Warhorse	8	3	–	3	3	1	3	1	5
Griffon	6	5	–	5	5	4	5	4	7
Imperial Pegasus	8	3	–	4	4	3	4	2	6
The Imperial Dragon	6	6	–	6	6	6	3	5	8

Special Rules

Griffons, Pegasi and the Imperial Dragon have wings that enable them to fly.

Griffons and the Imperial Dragon both cause Terror and are large targets.

The Imperial Dragon has a Strength 4 flaming breath weapon attack and scaly skin (3+).

STATE TROOPS AND MILITIA

Since the time of Sigmar, the Empire has maintained armies of professional soldiers who defend the Emperor's lands. Recruiting parties travel through the provinces, beating their drums and promising a life of adventure and glory for those who sign up to join the Emperor's armies. Drawn by love of their homeland or the promise of three meals a day, there are many men willing to risk life and limb in the state regiments of the Empire. State troops form the mainstay of the Empire's armies, though armies are often bulked out by ad hoc militia regiments recruited to fight as and when required (who will often be made up of mercenaries or local peasants levied from the surrounding lands). As well as forming a standing army, state troops serve as city guards and enforcers of local laws. In the case of the provinces, these forces fall under the command of the count, whereas in the city-states the city's Burgomeisters command them.

State Troops

State troops may be equipped in a variety of ways with different types of armour and weapons, but the most common weapon of an Empire soldier is the halberd,

a combination of spear and battleaxe that is wielded in both hands. Other regiments favour weapons such as handguns, swords or spears. A state regiment will often have smaller detachments of troops to support it, protecting its vulnerable flanks or showering the enemy with missile fire.

State troops wear the traditional colours of their province or city, with distinctive uniforms and mixes of badges, hats, medals or campaign symbols. There are no strict rules governing how these are worn, so it is common to find great variation between regiments, even those originating from the same town. Most soldiers wear some form of doublet and hose, with colourful undershirts pulled through slashes cut in the fabric of their jackets and britches. Other regiments wear plain tabards, decorated with their province or city's coat of arms. Despite such variations, each soldier will display his homeland's colours somewhere on his person. For example, a soldier of Middenland would include something blue in his uniform, perhaps wearing a blue jacket, tying off his britches with blue ribbons or simply sporting an enormous blue feather in his cap.

There are exceptions to this, of course, such as the Carroburg Greatwords (an infamously hard-bitten regiment who wear blood red uniforms despite hailing from the Reikland), the Death's Heads of the Ostermark and the Scarlet Guard of Stirland.

Halberdiers

A halberd is a long-hafted weapon with a heavy blade that is capable of smashing through heavy armour or the tough hides of creatures such as Orcs and Beastmen. Regiments of Halberdiers are the most numerous state soldiers, thanks to the Emperor's requirement that each Elector Count maintain a standing force of Halberdiers, but also due to their versatility and strength in battle.

Spearmen

Enemies who charge ranks of Spearmen are faced with a virtually impenetrable wall of lethal iron points. Spears are easy to manufacture and thus are more common in the northern and eastern provinces of the Empire where the constant threat of invasion requires battalions of soldiers to quickly be made battle ready.

Swordsmen

Swordsmen are expert blademasters, regarded as dashing, heroic figures who seek out the enemy's best warriors to prove their valour and skill. A skilled Swordsman can attack a foe's weak points while simultaneously defending himself with his shield.

Handgunners

These state troops are armed with long-barrelled black powder weapons known as handguns, often manufactured by the highly skilled gunsmiths of Nuln. The withering volleys of Handgunners' lead shot can break the most determined Orc Waaagh! or unhorse even a heavily armoured Chaos Knight.

Crossbowmen

Crossbows have a longer range than handguns and are far more easily produced, though they lack the penetrative power of handguns. Most Elector Counts retain a sizeable number of Crossbow regiments, while mercenary Crossbowmen (particularly those from Tilea) are frequently recruited to augment the firepower of an Empire army.

	M	WS	BS	S	T	W	I	A	Ld
Empire Halberdier	4	3	3	3	3	1	3	1	7
Empire Spearman	4	3	3	3	3	1	3	1	7
Sergeant	4	3	3	3	3	1	3	2	7
Empire Swordsman	4	4	3	3	3	1	4	1	7
Duellist	4	4	3	3	3	1	4	2	7
Empire Handgunner	4	3	3	3	3	1	3	1	7
Empire Crossbowman	4	3	3	3	3	1	3	1	7
Marksman	4	3	4	3	3	1	3	1	7

Special Rules

State Troops: State troops can be used as independent units, parent units or detachments. See the detachment rules on pages 38-39.

Militia

Militia are regiments recruited (willingly or not) to fight as required, and no one can foretell how many Men will answer the count's muster. Some of these troops will be grim mercenaries or Men used to living by the strength of their sword arm, while others will be peasants levied from the local countryside. These latter troops receive no training whatsoever and are armed with whatever weapons they own, be it bows, swords or cudgels. Some unscrupulous Elector Counts are known to throw militia regiments into the thickest fighting, knowing that dead mercenaries do not require paying...

Archers

Empire archers are normally organised into small groups of skirmishers who support the regimented units in battle. Trappers and hunters from the wilder, less 'civilised' provinces, such as Ostland and the Ostermark, are often called to serve in special units called Huntsmen. These masters of the wilderness scout ahead of the main body of the army to gather intelligence, disrupt enemy movements and pick off war machine crews with deadly accurate bowfire.

Free Companies

Roving bands of mercenaries or bandits returning from such wild and lawless places as the Border Princes or the Wasteland (or the untamed wilds of the Empire itself) are a plentiful source of irregular troops for an Elector Count. Battles in far-off lands have forged these Men into hardened warriors, but most are unable to settle back into normal society upon their return. They are hardy fighters and are well used to the rigours of war, but are uncouth, disreputable sorts, liable to cause trouble roaming around in dangerous, and often well-armed, bands. An Elector Count might seek to recruit these mercenaries for their skill in battle, but also to bring them under some sort of control and thus prevent brigandage going unchecked in his lands. Once the fighting is done, however, these Men are forcibly disbanded and dispersed before they become too unruly and begin plundering the lands they have just fought to protect.

	M	WS	BS	S	T	W	I	A	Ld
Empire Archer	4	3	3	3	3	1	3	1	7
Marksman	4	3	4	3	3	1	3	1	7
Free Company Fighter	4	3	3	3	3	1	3	1	7
Sergeant	4	3	3	3	3	1	3	2	7

Special Rules

Militia: Militia units can be used as independent units or detachments, but may not be parent units. See the detachment rules on pages 38-39.

Skirmishers: Archers are skirmishers, as described in the Warhammer rulebook.

Huntsmen: Archers upgraded to Huntsmen (see army list) have the scouts special rule.

The Detachment System

The soldiers of the Empire train every day to fight with specialised tactics that rely on their legendary discipline – the detachment system. Detachments are smaller regiments of troops that remain close to a parent unit in order to protect its vulnerable flanks and offer support, either by using missile weapons or by employing close combat weapons to threaten an enemy's exposed flanks. A favoured combination is to have two detachments supporting a parent unit, one armed with ranged weapons, the other armed with close combat weapons.

The detachment armed with missile weapons fires as the enemy advances – and should the enemy charge them, they will flee. This draws the attackers onto the blades of the close combat specialists or leaves them struggling in front of the main body of the regiment, ready to be charged in return.

Parent Units

Units of Halberdiers, Spearmen, Swordsmen, Crossbowmen and Handgunners may be used as independent units (ie, acting on their own, as normal), as parent units, and/or as detachments. Units of Archers, Huntsmen and Free Companies may not be used as parent units, but can be used as independent units or detachments. Greatswords may never be used as detachments, but can be used as an independent unit or a parent unit.

Detachments

- Each parent unit may have one or two detachments.

- Detachments do not count towards the minimum number of Core Troops choices.

- A Detachment's size can range from a minimum of five models (regardless of the unit's normal minimum) to a maximum of half the number of models in their parent unit, rounding down. Eg, 21 Halberdiers may have up to two detachments, each 5-10 men strong.

- Detachments cannot have a standard bearer, musician or champion.

- Detachments must be deployed simultaneously with their parent unit and within 3" of it.

- Detachments are normal units and are completely separate and independent from their parent unit (eg, they can choose to pursue a broken enemy while the parent unit holds its ground; spells and magic items affecting the parent unit do not affect its detachments; etc.).

- Detachments never cause Panic in any friendly unit (including other detachments), regardless of their unit strength.

- If a character joins a detachment, that detachment will be treated exactly like an independent unit (it will cause Panic in other Empire units if it is broken/fleeing/destroyed, etc.) and will not be able to use any of the detachment special rules for as long as the character stays with it.

Detachments in close support

To represent their unique way of fighting, detachments may use the following rules, but only if they are within 3" of their parent unit (and not if the parent unit is fleeing or has declared a flee reaction).

Use Parent Unit's Leadership

A detachment in close support (i.e. within 3" of its parent unit) always uses the parent unit's Leadership for any Leadership tests, unless its own Ld is higher (this could happen if the detachment is in range of the General's Leadership while the parent unit isn't, for example).

Support Fire *(figure 1)*

In the enemy's movement phase a detachment in close support may stand & shoot against an enemy unit charging its parent unit if the detachment itself has not been charged and is not countercharging in the same turn. A detachment can offer support fire even if the parent unit cannot stand & shoot itself (enemy too close, for example), and does not suffer the -1 to hit penalty for standing & shooting.

Countercharge *(figure 1)*

In the enemy's movement phase a detachment in close support may countercharge an enemy unit charging its parent unit if the detachment itself has not been charged. After the enemy has finished moving all its chargers, but before remaining moves, the detachment can declare a normal charge against the enemy. If the detachment can draw a line of sight to an exposed flank of the enemy, and has enough Movement to reach it, it can charge the enemy in the flank, even if it would normally have to charge its front. The detachment will get the normal flank attack combat bonus and will negate the enemy's rank bonus so long as the detachment has a unit strength of at least 5, as normal.

Apart from the exceptions noted above, the countercharge follows all the normal rules for charges (the detachment must pass a Leadership test to charge Fear-causing enemies, it can wheel only once during the move, etc.). In the close combat phase, resolve the countercharging detachment's attacks first, then resolve the attacks of the enemy and finally work out those of the parent unit that was charged.

Supporting Charge *(figure 2)*

In its own movement phase a detachment in close support may make a supporting charge by hitting the flank of an enemy unit charged in the front or rear by its parent unit (or indeed hitting the front or rear of an enemy unlucky enough to be charged in the flank by the parent unit). Declare the supporting charge when you declare the charge of the parent unit. If the charge of the parent unit does not hit its target (failed Psychology test, out of range, etc,), the detachment does not charge either, and may not move further nor shoot that turn. After the parent unit has been brought into contact with the target unit and after all other chargers have been moved, but before remaining moves, the detachment is moved into contact with the same target. If the detachment can draw a line of sight to an exposed flank of the target, and has enough Movement to reach it, it can charge the target's flank even if it should have charged its front. The detachment will get the normal flank attack combat bonus and will negate the enemy's rank bonus, so long as it has a unit strength of at least 5. Apart from the exceptions above, the supporting charge follows all the normal rules for charges.

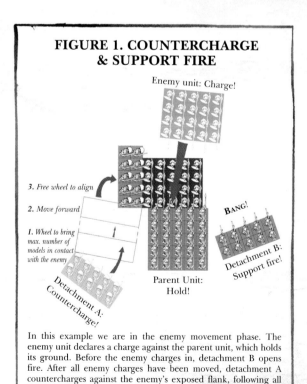

FIGURE 1. COUNTERCHARGE & SUPPORT FIRE

Enemy unit: Charge!

3. Free wheel to align

2. Move forward

1. Wheel to bring max. number of models in contact with the enemy

BANG!

Detachment B: Support fire!

Parent Unit: Hold!

Detachment A: Countercharge!

In this example we are in the enemy movement phase. The enemy unit declares a charge against the parent unit, which holds its ground. Before the enemy charges in, detachment B opens fire. After all enemy charges have been moved, detachment A countercharges against the enemy's exposed flank, following all the normal rules for moving chargers.

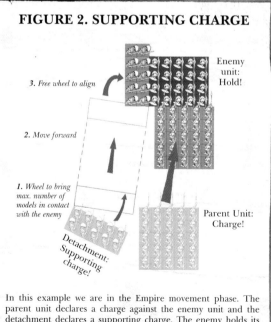

FIGURE 2. SUPPORTING CHARGE

Enemy unit: Hold!

3. Free wheel to align

2. Move forward

1. Wheel to bring max. number of models in contact with the enemy

Parent Unit: Charge!

Detachment: Supporting charge!

In this example we are in the Empire movement phase. The parent unit declares a charge against the enemy unit and the detachment declares a supporting charge. The enemy holds its ground. After all normal charges have been moved, the detachment charges the enemy's exposed flank (it does not matter if it is now beyond the 3" distance from its parent unit), following all the normal rules for moving chargers.

KNIGHTLY ORDERS

The Knightly Orders of the Empire are heroic brotherhoods of armoured warriors who ride into battle atop mighty barded warhorses. Knights are magnificent figures, clad in gleaming plate armour crafted by Dwarven smiths, armed with weaponry of the finest quality and mounted on powerful destriers. The thunderous charge of heavily armoured Knights is an awe-inspiring sight, their enemies spitted on the end of deadly lances or crushed beneath trampling hooves. Each Knight bears his Order's symbols upon his shield or armour, heraldic devices and icons of death that stretch back to the order's founding. Many sons of nobility choose to join one of the many brotherhoods located throughout the Empire and such Orders come in many different sizes. Some of these Knightly Orders, like the Knights Griffon, only recruit from the local nobility, while others become templars of a particular deity, such as the zealous Knights of Sigmar's Blood.

Knightly Orders are organised along strict lines of hierarchy, with each novice trained in martial virtue and the chivalric code until he is ready to take up the mantle of a fully-fledged Knight himself. The Order's veteran Knights form its inner circle, and these are the most powerful warriors in the Empire. When the courageous Knights of the Inner Circle go to war it is only to fight the most diabolical enemies, and their presence on the battlefield is worth many times their number.

Greater even than the Knights of the Inner Circle is the Grand Master, and it is he who commands the Knightly Order. The Grand Master is a warrior and leader of unparalleled valour, having fought in dozens of battles, and whose military prowess is beyond question. An Elector Count can request that a Knightly Order fight alongside his army, but the decision to ride out lies solely with the Grand Master.

This makes the Grand Master of a Knightly Order a very powerful individual, and a condition of his Order's aid may be that he himself takes command of the army. Most Elector Counts are only too happy for a general of such superlative ability to lead his soldiers, though this has not always proven to be the case, and ego, ambition or sheer lunacy has sometimes resulted in a Knightly Order withholding its aid.

The most famous Orders have histories stretching back centuries, their chapter houses hung with ancient banners first raised during the earliest days of the Empire when the Order's first warriors fought in the time of Sigmar.

Knights of the White Wolf

This fierce order of warriors are based in the northern city of Middenheim and follow the creed of Ulric, the god of battle, wolves and winter. The White Wolves wear mantles of wolfskin over their armour and eschew the use of a lance, instead carrying mighty cavalry hammers to smash the skulls of their foes. They carry no shields and disdain the wearing of helmets, to better display their long hair and beards and howl their ferocious war cries.

The Knights Panther

Knights Panther trace their origins to the terrible crusades against Araby and the defeat of Caliph Jaffar. The Sultan's warriors fashioned panther skulls into helmets and wore the hides of exotic beasts as cloaks. When Jaffar's army was defeated, one group of victorious Knights took the bloody pelts as trophies, hanging them from the pauldrons of their armour. Thus was born the Order of the Knights Panther, a courageous Order that is known and respected throughout the Empire.

HERTWIG'S FOLLY

At the Battle of Black Road Wolfram Hertwig, Elector Count of the Ostermark, stubbornly refused to allow the Grand Master of the Knights of the Everlasting Light to take command of his army, though Hertwig was barely into his teens and had never commanded an army in battle. In response, Grand Master Kessler and his warriors rode back to their chapter house, leaving Hertwig's army to fight the invading Orcs without their aid.

Though the greenskins were eventually defeated, the count's army suffered horrific losses and for many years, the Ostermark was dependant on aid from the armies of Ostland or Talabecland for its survival. Needless to say, Hertwig's Folly (as it has now become known) stands as a cautionary tale to those who would allow ego to blind them to the value of having the greatest warriors of the Empire fighting alongside them.

The Reiksguard

Founded at the time of the ascension of the Reik Princes to the Empire's throne, the Reiksguard are sworn to protect the life of the Emperor. As the best troops available to the Emperor, the Reiksguard form the core of the Imperial household guard, both on the field of battle as well as at other, more stately, functions. Their Grand Master is known as the Reiksmarshal, and he is second only to the Emperor himself in matters of war. Imperial history is rich with records of decisive battles won by a timely charge by the Reiksguard. Despite the potential power and influence that such a reputation offers, the Reiksguard has stayed apolitical, loyal first, last and always to the reigning Emperor.

The Knights of the Blazing Sun

This Order of Knights was also formed during the Crusades against Araby, after the Battle of Magritta. During fierce fighting around the temple of the warrior goddess Myrmidia, a group of Knights were trapped by the dreaded Black Guard of Emir Wasr the Cruel. As the Arabyans closed in, a mighty earthquake shook the temple and a huge bronze statue of the goddess plummeted to the street, crushing the Emir and his troops. Seeing this as a sign from the heavens, the Knights drove their enemies from the field of battle. Shortly thereafter, the surviving Knights established the Order of the Blazing Sun with Myrmidia as its patron and protector. Upon returning to the Empire, they built a shrine to Myrmidia in the heart of Talabheim. Though many folk mistrust them for their courting of strange foreign deities, the Knights of the Blazing Sun have fought with distinction against the enemies of the Emperor and are held as a prized ally by many Elector Counts.

	M	WS	BS	S	T	W	I	A	Ld
Templar Grand Master	4	6	3	4	4	3	6	4	9
Inner Circle Preceptor	4	4	3	4	3	1	3	2	8
Inner Circle Knight	4	4	3	4	3	1	3	1	8
Preceptor	4	4	3	3	3	1	3	2	8
Knight	4	4	3	3	3	1	3	1	8
Warhorse	8	3	3	3	3	1	3	1	5

Equipment

Full Plate Armour: Knights ride into battle wearing all-enclosing suits of armour, crafted by Dwarven smiths and kept in great honour in the armouries of the chapter house. Such armour is very rare, but offers the best protection available to the warriors of Mankind. Full plate armour gives a 4+ armour save.

Special Rules

Master of Battle: Templar Grand Masters are veterans of hundreds of battles and are so strong in their faith, that they are Immune to Psychology. In addition, if a Templar Grand Master joins a unit of Knights of his own Order then they are so inspired by his presence that they too are Immune to Psychology so long as he remains with the unit.

PISTOLIERS AND OUTRIDERS

Pistoliers

Regiments of Pistoliers are recruited from the younger sons of Empire nobles eager to win their spurs as Knights and for whom the clarion call to arms pounds in their veins. Some may gather their friends and form regiments of their own, but most join the ranks of the Pistolkorps, a semi-formal organisation funded by the Emperor, College of Engineers and several Knightly Orders. Here the nobles learn about horsemanship and war from the Outriders – grizzled veterans paid by the knights to train their sons – before being judged worthy to join a Knightly Order.

In battle, Pistoliers act as light cavalry who gallop around the enemy flanks, disrupting formations and launching devastating hit-and-run attacks with their pistols blazing. Equipped from the treasuries of their families, each Pistolier cuts a dashing figure with his flamboyant livery, plumed helmet and brace of pistols.

Since most Pistoliers are young, inexperienced and hungry for personal glory, they tend to be hot-headed and impetuous, charging off into battle where more cautious soldiers might bide their time. Such fiery courage is only to be expected of Pistoliers and indulging it is seen as a good way of tempering their wildness into something more dependable.

	M	WS	BS	S	T	W	I	A	Ld
Pistolier	4	3	3	3	3	1	3	1	7
Outrider	4	3	4	3	3	1	3	1	7
Warhorse	8	3	–	3	3	1	3	1	5

Special Rules
Fast Cavalry.

Outriders

Most of the young men who survive their time in the Pistoliers go on to join a Knightly Order and put the skills and scars they have earned to good use as a fully armoured Knight. Others, for whom the thrill and excitement of life in the Pistoliers is too hard to relinquish, stay with their regiment or go on to become drill instructors in the Pistolkorps.

These men typically wear more ornate armour and tend to sport eccentrically waxed moustaches to better differentiate themselves from their younger charges. These older, wiser riders frequently lead the headstrong Pistoliers into battle. At other times they form separate regiments of Outriders for the College of Engineers, each equipped with deadly repeater handguns, weapons capable of unleashing devastating storms of lead at long range. The leader of the Outriders will often be armed with an even more outlandish weapon as befits his status, gifted to him by a patron Engineer.

	M	WS	BS	S	T	W	I	A	Ld
Outrider	4	3	4	3	3	1	3	1	7
Outrider Champion	4	3	5	3	3	1	3	1	7
Warhorse	8	3	–	3	3	1	3	1	5

Special Rules
Fast Cavalry.

GREATSWORDS

Members of the Greatswords are grim men who fight with massive, two-handed blades that can cleave an armoured Knight in twain with one blow. Clad in magnificent, gleaming suits of Dwarf-forged plate armour, only the bravest and most honourable soldiers are ever promoted to the ranks of the Greatswords. These are Men who have earned such an honour in the thick of the bloodiest and most heroic fighting, accomplishing incredible feats of arms before their commanding officers. Though this is incredibly dangerous, there is no shortage of those willing to risk their lives for the chance to be raised to such a respected position. On one occasion during the Battle of Blood Ridge, Albrecht Hoefner, the last survivor of von Menscher's Blackhelms, received his promotion after defending his regiment's colours for an entire day against repeated attacks from scores of bloodthirsty tribesmen and mutated beasts. It is the dream of almost every soldier in the Empire to serve in a regiment of Greatswords, but it is a dream that few Men have the courage or skill to realise.

The Greatswords garrison the castles of the Elector Counts and form their personal bodyguard on the battlefield. Each soldier is required to swear an oath never to take a backward step in the face of the enemy, and each regiment of Greatswords has its own particular punishments for those who fail in their duty. Such instances are extremely rare and the history of the Empire is replete with heroic tales of regiments of Greatswords that have died to a man to protect the life of their liege lord. Such devotion is well rewarded, as Greatswords receive double pay, eat the best food and live in well-appointed barracks within the castle walls. Especially heroic Greatswords may even be knighted by the Elector Count, a rare honour for a soldier raised from the ranks.

	M	WS	BS	S	T	W	I	A	Ld
Count's Champion	4	4	3	3	3	1	3	2	8
Greatsword	4	4	3	3	3	1	3	1	8

Equipment

Full Plate Armour: Greatswords are equipped with magnificent suits of plate armour that are said to have been crafted by Dwarven smiths. Each soldier is required to care for his own armour and takes great pride in the embellishments and ostentation of his suit of armour. Full plate armour gives a 4+ armour save.

Special Rules

Stubborn: Greatswords are Men of the finest character who swear mighty oaths never to retreat in the face of the enemy. All Greatswords are Stubborn, as described in the Warhammer rulebook.

State Troops: Greatswords can be used either as independent units or parent units, but not as detachments. See the rules on pages 38-39.

THE CARROBURG GREATSWORDS

The Carroburg Greatswords are one of the most famous regiments in the Empire, with tales of their valour and ruthlessness told from Marienburg to Talabheim. The regiment earned its bloody reputation after the Siege of Carroburg in 1865, where its soldiers successfully defended the walls of their city against the Count of Middenland's vast army. Despite the horrific casualties and many wounds they suffered during the battle, the Greatswords fought on resolutely and by battle's end, their white Reikland uniforms were drenched in blood. From that moment onwards, the Carroburg Greatswords have worn dark red uniforms in remembrance of that bloody battle.

BATTLE WIZARDS

Wizards are strange figures who wield awesome magical powers and are privy to secrets usually beyond the ken of normal folk. Trained at the Colleges of Magic for many years, arcane power courses through their veins and lurks behind their eyes like the thunder before a storm. No sane inhabitant of the Empire willingly courts the attention of a Wizard, for they are unpredictable and (some whisper) tainted by the very magic they wield. The services of a Wizard are much sought after by the Elector Counts, as many of their enemies employ potent shamans or fell sorcerers. Such foes bend the Winds of Magic to evil and destructive ends and only those skilled in the arcane arts may stand against such power.

Battle Wizards hurl bolts of fire and lightning at the foe, confound them with illusions or steal away their courage. Each of the Lores of Magic has the power to smite the enemies of the Empire and it is a rare army that marches to war without at least one Battle Wizard. To be a Wizard is to understand the power at the heart of the world and though each can bend one of the eight Winds of Magic to his will, such power is not wielded lightly. To lose control of such dangerous power would be to damn one's soul to an eternity of torment at the hands of the Dark Gods themselves…

	M	WS	BS	S	T	W	I	A	Ld
Wizard Lord	4	3	3	3	4	3	3	1	8
Wizard	4	3	3	3	3	2	3	1	7

Empire Wizards may choose their spells from any one of the Lores of Magic that are presented in the Warhammer rulebook.

CANNONS AND MORTARS

The Gunnery School casts nearly every artillery piece employed by the Emperor's armies. It is a gigantic complex of mighty forges and the Elector Counts spend much of their wealth to acquire the Gunnery School's finest artillery pieces and to have their artillerymen trained by its gunnery captains.

Great Cannons

The cannons of the Gunnery School are the terror of the Empire's foes. Thunderous cannon fire sends iron balls hammering into the ranks of enemy warriors, each impact ploughing bloody furrows through tightly packed regiments. Even the mightiest creature cannot ignore the power of a Great Cannon, as was ably demonstrated at the Siege of Middenheim, when Master Gunner Pumhart von Steyr decapitated a rampaging Dragon with a single well-placed shot.

	M	WS	BS	S	T	W	I	A	Ld
Great Cannon	-	-	-	-	7	3	-	-	-
Crewman	4	3	3	3	3	1	3	1	7

A Great Cannon follows the rules for war machines that are presented in the Warhammer rulebook.

Mortars

More squat than Great Cannons, Mortars lob shells high into the air, which then fall amongst the enemy. Instead of solid shot, Mortars fire hollow shells topped with a fizzing fuse and filled with black-powder. Shells explode in the heart of a target regiment, sending fragments of burning iron scything through enemy ranks and killing whole swathes of warriors at once.

	M	WS	BS	S	T	W	I	A	Ld
Mortar	-	-	-	-	7	3	-	-	-
Crewman	4	3	3	3	3	1	3	1	7

	Strength	Wounds Caused	Armour Save
Normal hit	3	1	-1
Under the hole	6	D3	none

A Mortar follows the rules for war machines that are presented in the Warhammer rulebook.

Firing the Mortar

Pivot the Mortar so it is pointing in the direction you wish to fire and the crew can see the target. Declare how far you want to fire the mortar shell, without measuring, and guessing the range as accurately as you can. You must guess a distance of between 12" and 48". After guessing, place the centre of the large 5" template over the spot you have guessed.

To see where the shell lands roll both the scatter dice and the artillery dice. If the scatter dice rolls a HIT then the shell lands exactly on target. If the scatter dice rolls an arrow then the shell veers off in the direction of the arrow. If you roll a number on the artillery dice, this is the distance in inches the shell veers off target as shown by the arrow on the scatter dice. Move the template the distance indicated in the direction shown by the arrow. If a HIT was rolled on the scatter dice then the numbers are ignored. If the artillery dice rolls a MISFIRE then something has gone wrong – roll a D6 and consult the Mortar misfire chart below. A misfire roll automatically cancels out the whole shot regardless of the scatter dice result.

Damage

Models hit by the shell take one Strength 3 hit with a -1 armour save modifier that causes 1 wound. Single models directly under the template's central hole are always hit, even their base is not entirely covered. A model under the hole takes a Strength 6 hit that causes D3 wounds, with no armour save allowed.

MORTAR MISFIRE CHART

D6	Result
1	**Boom!** The mortar shell explodes before it is fired. The Mortar and crew are destroyed.
2-3	**Dud.** The fuse fizzles and the gun fails to fire. It takes a complete turn to replace the shell, so the Mortar cannot shoot this turn or next turn.
4-6	**Short Fuse.** The shell explodes in mid air, so the shot has no effect this turn.

MASTER ENGINEERS

Founded over five hundred years ago, the Imperial College of Engineers was the brainchild of Leonardo of Miragliano, a mad genius from the fractious land of Tilea, and his patron, the Prince of Altdorf. This institution attracted many forward thinking individuals, eager to develop the new science of engineering. Over the years, the college has grown larger, even attracting renegade Dwarf engineers cast from their halls for attempting to 'improve' tried and tested Dwarf technology.

Though much of an Engineer's time is spent tinkering with half-finished inventions of whimsy, each recognises that the ultimate purpose of their labours is coming up with new ideas to combat the multifarious threats to the Empire. Anti-flyer weapons, tunnelling machines, ice rays, alchemical bombs and all manner of weird devices are but a handful of the deadly inventions devised by the Engineers. They are eccentric individuals, muttering incomprehensible gobbledygook and bustling from one machine to another to improve its performance. While they are not soldiers, Engineers are often found on the battlefield, taking advantage of the fighting to field-test their latest inventions or snipe at the enemy with a variety of powerful experimental handguns.

The contraptions Engineers bring to battle range from utterly lethal devices, such as the Helblaster Volley Gun, to the downright bizarre, such as von Hugon's Terror Bell, the Thunder Barrel or the Herstel-Wenckler Pigeon Bomb. In addition, some Engineers oversee the army's artillery pieces, baffling the gunners with talk of parabolic arcs and making last minute adjustments to ensure that each weapon functions perfectly. Though no self-respecting gunner would ever admit that a bookworm could improve on years of experience behind a gun, the presence of an Engineer actually does make artillery more accurate.

	M	WS	BS	S	T	W	I	A	Ld
Master Engineer	4	3	4	3	3	2	3	1	7

Special Rules

Master of Ballistics: A Great Cannon or Mortar (not a Helstorm Rocket Battery or a Helblaster Volley Gun – weapons still too experimental for anyone to be an expert with) that an Engineer has joined may re-roll either one scatter dice or one artillery dice per turn. This, however, may not be the roll to determine the distance bounced by a cannonball – Engineers are good, but not that good! If the Engineer uses his re-roll ability during the firing of the war machine he has joined, he cannot shoot with his own missile weapon in the same shooting phase. Remember to fire all guess range weapons before any normal shooting!

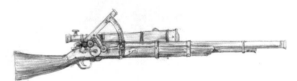

Extra Crewman: An Engineer can also replace one crew member of a war machine he joins, including Volley Guns (which will fire using the Engineer's Ballistic Skill) and Rocket Batteries, but if the Engineer is operating the machine, he cannot fire his own missile weapon. If a machine with an Engineer attached to it explodes, the Engineer will be killed with the rest of the crew if he replaced a crewman or used his re-roll ability during that turn (ie, if he was too close to the gun when it exploded!).

Experimental Weaponry

The items in the following list are some of the more 'reliable' experimental creations of the Engineers and can be chosen by them (and certain fortunate others...) according to the specific entries given in the army list section of this book.

Hochland Long Rifle

Leon Tödmeister's Fantabulously Far-reaching Harquebus of Unforeseeable and Unperceived Bereavement.

The Hochland long rifle was developed from weapons used by the hunters of that land and is the terror of enemy commanders and unit leaders.

Maximum Range: 36"; **Strength:** 4.

Special Rules: Move-or-fire; armour piercing.

Scientific Precision. The shooter may pick any target he can see (including characters or champions within a unit, a war machine's crew, on a chariot, riding a monster, etc,), but if he uses this special ability he will suffer a -1 to hit. The normal -1 modifier for shooting at a single Man-sized model does not apply (but other modifiers do) and a character/champion cannot benefit from the "Look Out, Sir!" rule. The shooter may choose a different target from the one chosen by the unit he is with.

Repeater Handgun

Von Meinkopt's Whirling Cavalcade of Death.

The repeater handgun is a recent innovation, a deadly weapon with a high rate of fire.

Maximum range: 24"; **Strength:** 4.

Special Rules: 3 x multiple shots; armour piercing; move or fire.

Repeater Pistol

Von Meinkopt's Micro-mainspring of Multitudinous Precipitation of Pernicious Lead.

The repeater pistol is a very effective side arm.

Maximum range: 8"; **Strength:** 4.

Special Rules: 3 x multiple shots; (4x multiple shots if combined with a pistol); armour piercing; always stand & shoot. A repeater pistol counts as a hand weapon in close combat.

Grenade Launching Blunderbuss

Pfielmann's Incendiary Projector of Explosive Misfortune.

Developed by taking the concept of the gamekeeper's blunderbuss and marrying it to the technologies of pistons and explosives, this weapon was designed to knock out heavily armoured enemy Knights.

Maximum Range: 16"; **Strength:** 6.

Special Rules: armour piercing; move or fire.

Mechanical Steed

Meikle's Equine Effigy of Dynamic Locomotion.

In order to create her 'carriageless horse', Frau Meikle – the first woman to be (somewhat reluctantly) admitted to the College of Engineers – built this mechanical marvel in conjunction with her frazzled assistant. The machine's legs are linked to an accumulator which is in turn connected to a pair of brass globes attached to the 'horse's' head. When the contraption charges into battle, the Engineer mounted upon it can unleash this stored energy as a lightning arc powerful enough to roast the foe alive.

	M	WS	BS	S	T	W	I	A	Ld
Mechanical Steed	8	1	–	4	4	1	1	1	–

Special Rules: A model mounted on a mechanical steed counts as riding a barded Warhorse (+2 armour save, -1" movement). In addition, if the model charges, the brass globes release a burst of lightning that does D3 impact hits with a Strength of 4.

Pigeon Bombs

Herstel-Wenckler Pigeon Bomb.

The Engineers have succeeded in training a determined cadre of homing pigeons to fly away from the carrier and towards the oncoming foe. Each bird is fitted with a bomb on a light metal harness, designed to fall away from the bird when the fuse burns to a certain point.

Maximum range: unlimited; **Strength:** 4.

Special Rules: 3" round template; move-or-fire.

Pigeon Bomb: Pigeon bombs are a missile weapon with the profile above. Nominate any enemy model visible to the Master Engineer, roll a D6 and consult the chart below.

PIGEON BOMB CHART

D6	Result
1	**Oops!** The confused pigeon returns to its handler! Place the template over the Master Engineer and resolve the explosion.
2-4	**Boom!** A poorly cut fuse means the bomb explodes harmlessly in mid air (harmlessly for everyone except for the pigeon!).
5-6	**Huzzah!** The pigeon lands exactly on the head of the right target. Place the template over the target model and resolve the explosion.

HELBLASTER VOLLEY GUN

The Helblaster Volley Gun is one of the most infamous black-powder weapons ever invented, its devastating firepower able to tear apart an entire regiment in one thunderous volley. The lethal creation of the deranged Engineer von Meinkopt, its terrifying reputation has spread to all corners of the Old World. Its nine separate barrels are divided into three 'decks' and are turned by means of a central crank, which means that it can unleash devastating hails of shot that engulf its unfortunate target in a firestorm of leaden death. Even heavily armoured Chaos Warriors can be shredded by a single volley, though with such devastating power comes great risk. Helblaster Volley Guns are notoriously prone to sudden, cataclysmic explosions. As a result, those crewmen who operate a machine so prone to catastrophically blowing them to tiny pieces tend to be paid up with the priests of Morr.

	M	WS	BS	S	T	W	I	A	Ld
Helblaster	–	–	–	–	7	3	–	–	–
Crewman	4	3	3	3	3	1	3	1	7

Range	Hits/Shot	Strength	Armour Save
24"	Artillery dice	5	-3

A Volley Gun follows the rules for war machines in the Warhammer rulebook.

Firing the Volley Gun

The Volley Gun has a range of 24". Nominate your target and turn the Volley Gun to face it. Then fire the first barrel. The barrel will fire a variable number of shots equal to the roll of an artillery dice. Once you have fired the first barrel, shoot the second barrel at the same target and then the third. The final total is the number of shots fired by the Volley Gun.

If you roll a misfire result on any of the artillery dice, consult the Volley Gun misfire chart and apply the result immediately. Then roll the artillery dice for any remaining barrels (assuming you still can!). You must fire all three barrels when shooting the Volley Gun, even if the target is found to be out of range.

Measure the range to the target and roll to hit as normal for the shots that have been fired, applying all normal to-hit modifiers.

VOLLEY GUN MISFIRE CHART

D6	Result
1	**Destroyed!** The Volley Gun explodes with a mighty crack. Resolve any shots fired by previous barrels in this group and then remove the Volley Gun and its crew.
2-3	**Jammed.** The firing mechanism and the main crank grind to a halt. Any remaining shots in this group of three barrels are wasted and the crew must spend the following turn unjamming the machine.
4	**Malfunction.** The firing mechanism blocks and the barrel does not fire. In addition, any remaining shots in this group of three barrels are wasted. You can fire as normal in the next shooting phase.
5	**Dud.** The powder fails to ignite and the barrel does not fire. However, you can continue to fire any remaining barrels in this group of three as normal.
6	**KA-BOOM!** The barrel you were rolling for and any remaining barrels in this group all fire 10 shots. After resolving the shots, the Volley Gun is destroyed and its crew slain. Remove the Volley Gun and its crew.

HELSTORM ROCKET BATTERY

After watching the spectacular fireworks of a Cathayan emissary to Altdorf, Master Engineer Herman Faulkstein was inspired to transform this eastern technology into a weapon. His early research blew apart entire laboratories of the College of Engineers while he attempted to discover the secrets of rocket-powered flight, but the permanently soot-blackened Engineer never lost faith that his designs had a military value.

Faulkstein's original rockets were wildly inaccurate; madly corkscrewing weapons that had no chance whatsoever of hitting anything other than (eventually) the ground. Further refinements such as fins, long sticks added to the base of a rocket and a launch carriage to direct the early portion of its flight further improved stability and accuracy – though neither were particularly impressive. However, when the rockets did manage to land on target, the results were devastating, with entire enemy regiments blown apart by an earth-shaking cascade of shrieking, explosive rockets. After the Elector Count of Middenland was almost blown to smithereens by an errant volley of rockets (though he was nowhere near the intended target) they were dubbed 'Helstorm' rockets after the colourful language used by the count on the unfortunate Engineer.

	M	WS	BS	S	T	W	I	A	Ld
Rocket Battery	–	–	–	–	7	3	–	–	–
Crewman	4	3	3	3	3	1	3	1	7

Range	Strength	Wounds caused	Armour Save
12"-48"	5	1	-2

A Helstorm Rocket Battery follows the rules for war machines in the Warhammer rulebook.

Firing the Rocket Battery

Nominate the target model and turn the Rocket Battery to face it. Declare how far you want to fire the salvo of rockets, guessing the range without measuring. You must guess a distance between 12" and 48".

Once you've made your guess, roll the artillery dice. If the artillery dice shows a misfire, something has gone wrong – roll a D6 and consult the rocket misfire chart. A misfire roll automatically cancels out the shot. If the artillery dice shows a number, add the result of the artillery dice to the amount you guessed and then place the 5" round template this many inches from the Rocket Battery.

Now roll the scatter dice and an artillery dice (again). If you roll a hit, then the rocket salvo lands on target. If you roll an arrow, move the template the number of inches indicated by the artillery dice (re-rolling any misfire results on this second roll).

Damage

Each model hit by the rocket salvo takes a Strength 5 hit with the normal -2 armour save modifier. Any single model directly under the template's hole is automatically hit, even if its base is not completely covered.

ROCKET MISFIRE CHART

D6   Result

1   **Boom!** The rocket explodes on the launch rails before it is fired. The Rocket Battery and crew are destroyed.

2   **Oops!** The rockets spiral out of control before coming to land in the Empire lines. Centre the template on the Rocket Battery and roll both the scatter and artillery dice (re-rolling misfires) to see where the errant rockets land.

3-4   **Dud.** The fuses fizzles out and the rockets fail to fire. It takes a complete turn to replace the rockets, so the battery cannot shoot this turn or next turn either.

5-6   **Short Fuse.** The rockets explode in mid air, so the shot has no effect this turn.

STEAM TANK

Steam Tanks are monstrous, smoke-belching creations that rumble towards the enemy, firing deadly cannonballs from their steam-powered guns. The advance of these iron behemoths is terrifying to behold, as arrows ricochet from armoured hulls and enemy warriors are crushed beneath their immense bulk. Powered by a pressurised boiler that siphons steam through pipes and pistons, the Steam Tank is the inspired design of the famed Leonardo of Miragliano. Twelve Steam Tanks were originally built, though only eight now remain, carefully maintained by the College of Engineers. In times of war, the College may sanction the use of these rare and valuable machines should the threat be dire enough.

In battle, the Engineer Commander of a Steam Tank directs the pressurised steam to whichever portion of the tank requires it, be it the pistons that drive the wheels or the tank's steam-powered weapons. It is a delicate art to judge how much pressure the boiler can hold, but the higher the pressure, the more options the Commander has at his disposal. Should too much pressure build, then the boiler may rupture with catastrophic effect!

Most Steam Tanks are armed with a steam-powered cannon, which is smaller than the cannons of the Imperial Gunnery School, though the manoeuvrability of the Steam Tank compensates for this. A turret-mounted steam gun is also standard, and this innovative weapon douses enemy close to the tank in a blast of scalding steam.

	M	WS	BS	S	T	W	I	A	Ld
Steam Tank	special	–	–	6	6	10	–	special	–
Engineer Commander	–	–	4	–	–	–	–	–	10

Armour save 1+.

Except where noted otherwise, a Steam Tank counts as a war machine in all respects.

Equipment
The Steam Tank is armed with a main cannon in the hull and a steam gun in the turret. The Engineer Commander is armed with a repeater pistol.

Special Rules
A Steam Tank is a large target, Unbreakable and causes Terror. A Steam Tank has a unit strength of 10.

Building up Steam Points

At the start of your turn, declare how many steam points (SP) the Steam Tank is attempting to generate, ie, how much pressure the Engineer is allowing to build up in the boiler. This can be any number between 0 and 5 SP. It's a good idea to use a dice near the Steam Tank to represent how many SP it has, turning it over each time you use one.

If you declared 1 or more SP, roll a D6 and add the number of steam points you've decided to generate. If the total is equal to or less than the Steam Tank's remaining Wounds, all is well. If the total is greater, then something has gone wrong. The Steam Tank loses one Wound and no SP are generated that turn. If you decide to generate no SP then you do not need to roll the D6, but the Steam Tank can do nothing that turn – though the Engineer may shoot his repeater pistol as normal.

Using Steam Points

Steam points can be used during the movement phase to move the tank, in the shooting phase to fire its guns or in the close combat phase to grind opponents into a bloody mess. All unused SP are lost at the end of the turn, so use as many as you can!

Movement phase

The Steam Tank moves in the same manner as a chariot, with each SP allowing you to move it 3". However, the Steam Tank does not double its movement distance when it charges. All difficult terrain counts as impassable terrain, but obstacles present no challenge to its bulk and have no effect on a Steam Tank. Any obstacles should be removed after the tank has passed through them.

To charge with a Steam Tank, first declare charges as normal (i.e. the tank needs to be able to see the target in its front arc of sight) and specify how many SP you are using to charge with. The target unit may make a charge reaction, as normal. If the Steam Tank fails to reach its target, it is moved its full Movement allowance towards the target (this is not halved). If the Steam Tank hits its target, it does D3 impact hits, plus an extra D3 for each SP used for the charge.

Magic phase

The Steam Tank's metal mass is enough to scramble and block most magical attacks. Only spells with a given Strength can damage Steam Tanks – all other spell effects are ignored.

Shooting phase

Once per turn, the Steam Tank may fire its hull-mounted cannon against visible targets in its frontal arc. This costs 2 SP and can be done even if the tank has moved or is in close combat. The cannon shot is worked out as described in the rules for cannons in the Warhammer rulebook. If you roll a misfire on the first artillery dice, the Steam Tank suffers D3 Wounds and the cannonball is not fired.

Main Cannon

Range	Strength	Wounds caused	Armour Save	Notes
18"	8	D3	No save	Cannon

Note that the main cannon cannot fire grapeshot, but any unit in base contact with the front of the tank when the cannon fires automatically suffers D3 S2 hits with no armour save from the escaping steam. Then resolve the cannon's shot as normal.

In addition, once per turn the tank may shoot its steam gun at any target within a 360° fire arc at a cost of 1 SP. Place the flame template on the end of the steam gun. Models fully covered by the template are hit automatically, while those whose bases are partially covered are hit on a 4+.

Steam Gun

Range	Strength	Armour Save
Teardrop template	2	No save

Both these weapons can be fired in close combat and can even be fired against the unit the tank is in close combat with, provided there is no chance of hitting friendly models or enemy models that are in base contact with friendly models other than the tank. Remember, the tank is a large target and so it can see over models that are not large targets, even when engaged in close combat.

If the Steam Tank is not engaged in close combat, then the Engineer can open the hatch and fire his repeater pistol with a 360° fire arc at the same or a different target to the Steam Tank. He will not risk himself in close combat, but can make a stand & shoot reaction before ducking back inside. This is the only permitted charge reaction for a Steam Tank.

Close Combat phase

A Steam Tank engaged in close combat may grind its opponents by expending SP. Each expended SP inflicts D3 impact hits. Opponents in close combat automatically hit the Steam Tank and roll to wound normally. A Steam Tank cannot overrun or pursue.

Impact Hits against the Steam Tank

Units that cause impact hits against the Steam Tank do so as normal, but suffer D6 S6 hits themselves.

Characteristic Tests

A Steam Tank will automatically pass any characteristic test it is required to make, with the exception of Initiative tests, which it automatically fails (not being too good at dodging).

WARRIOR PRIESTS OF SIGMAR

Sigmar is a warrior god, and to follow his creed is to live a life of battle. The Cult of Sigmar demands that its followers must fight all forms of evil with strength of arm and sword as well as faith, and many of its priests accompany the Empire's armies as they march to war. In this role they not only lead and inspire troops in battle, but also minister to their spiritual well-being. On many occasions, a rousing speech or tour of camp by a Warrior Priest of Sigmar has restored faith, brought hope or stayed mutiny when the words of even the most respected general has fallen on deaf ears.

Throughout the Empire it is considered only right and proper to honour all the gods, and even the priests of a particular deity show respect to other gods in appropriate situations. Where the older gods are seen to care little for Humans, Sigmar is the patron of

the Empire and of its people – which is why the inhabitants of the Empire call themselves Sigmar's People. This is true throughout the Empire – even in places where Ulric, Taal and other gods are the most actively worshipped.

The High Priest of the Cult of Sigmar is the Grand Theogonist, and beneath him are his two Arch Lectors. In these dark times, the practice of malign sorcery, the curse of undeath and the worship of Chaos infest the Empire and it is the duty of Arch Lectors and their clerics, the Warrior Priests, to destroy such evils. Arch Lectors are imposing figures, clad in ceremonial vestments and armour adorned with the Holy Hammer and twin-tailed comet of Sigmar. Their prayers are calls to war, their hymns the clash of arms and their benedictions the smiting of enemies with mighty warhammers.

Almost every town and village in the Empire has at least one shrine to Sigmar and thus Warrior Priests are a common sight throughout the Emperor's realm. In battle, the power of Sigmar stirs within their breast and divine might is theirs to command, allowing them to perform miracles in the name of their god. A Priest of Sigmar can unleash his wrath to smite creatures of darkness, call upon divine protection or return a wounded comrade from the brink of death.

To see such signs of Sigmar's favour fires the hearts of Men, and all who witness such miracles redouble their efforts to defeat their enemies. Woe betide the foe that must face an army filled with the power of Sigmar!

	M	WS	BS	S	T	W	I	A	Ld
Arch Lector	4	4	3	4	4	3	4	2	9
Warrior Priest	4	4	3	4	4	2	4	2	8

Special Rules

Blessings of Sigmar: Priests of Sigmar (ie, Warrior Priests and Arch Lectors) can invoke their patron god's protection against the sorcerous powers of the enemy. So long as he is on the battlefield and is not fleeing, a Priest of Sigmar adds a number of dice to the Empire player's dispel dice pool during the enemy's magic phase. A Warrior Priest adds one dice to the dispel dice pool, while an Arch Lector adds two.

Righteous Fury: Priests of Sigmar use rousing oratory to inflame the passions and stir a bitter hatred of the enemy. The Priest and any unit he joins Hate all models in the enemy army, so long as he remains with the unit. This does not affect characters, who are more difficult to influence than the average soldier.

Prayers of Sigmar: Priests of Sigmar are granted exceptional powers by their divine patron which they can wield to smite their foes in battle. Once per magic phase, a Priest of Sigmar is allowed to use prayers from the Prayers of Sigmar list opposite. An Arch Lector may use two different prayers per turn and a Warrior Priest may use one. Prayers are cast exactly like bound spells with a power level of 4. Unless differently stated in their description, they can be cast on the Priest himself or on any one character or unit champion within 12" of the Priest.

The War Altar of Sigmar

When war calls the High Priests of Sigmar to battle, it is an awe-inspiring sight to see them ride at the head of an army atop the mighty War Altar of Sigmar. Fashioned in the time of Magnus the Pious, the War Altar is a colossal chariot, ornate and gleaming with a towering effigy of a golden griffon carried upon it. The griffon was the symbol of Magnus and is a source of raw magic, seething with potent energies that a High Priest of Sigmar can draw upon to devastating effect. Against the forces of Chaos, where the danger of spiritual malaise and moral corruption is as great a danger as death, the Grand Theogonist may despatch

---

PRAYERS OF SIGMAR

Hammer of Sigmar: The model can re-roll failed rolls to hit and wound. Remains in play.

Armour of Contempt: The model gets a 4+ ward save. Remains in play.

Healing Hand: The model is immediately healed of all the wounds it has suffered during the battle up to that moment.

Unbending Righteousness: Can only be cast on the Priest himself. The Priest and any unit he joins is Unbreakable. If the Priest leaves the unit or is slain, the prayer will immediately cease to affect the unit. Remains in play.

Soulfire: Can only be cast on the Priest himself. All enemy units in base contact with the Priest suffer D6 Strength 4 hits with no armour saves allowed. Undead, Daemon or Forest Spirit units suffer D6 Strength 5 hits with no armour saves allowed.

---

one of his Arch Lectors to do battle from the back of the War Altar. Bellowing unforgiving verses from the Canticle of the Heldenhammer, the Arch Lector imbues the army's soldiers with a profound and righteous fury, his inspirational presence shielding their souls against the manifold horrors that the world throws at them.

	M	WS	BS	S	T	W	I	A	Ld
The War Altar	–	–	–	5	5	5	–	–	–
Warhorse	8	3	–	3	–	–	3	1	5

Armour save 5+.

The War Altar is a chariot drawn by two barded Warhorses.

Special Rules

The War Altar is a large target and has a unit strength of 5.

The Power of Sigmar: The divine protection of Sigmar makes both the War Altar and the Arch Lector Unbreakable. It also confers magic resistance (2) and a 4+ ward save on both the War Altar and the Arch Lector.

The Golden Griffon: The Arch Lector may unleash the power contained within the indomitable form of the golden griffon. Once per Empire magic phase, the griffon allows the Arch Lector to cast any one spell from the Lore of Light (see the Warhammer rulebook), which is cast at power level 5, exactly like a bound spell.

FLAGELLANT WARBANDS

The terrible plagues and wars of recent years, combined with prophecies of the Lord of the End Times and the doom of the world, has filled the hearts of the Empire's people with despair and hopelessness. In the wake of such calamities come hardship and terror as death stalks the landscape and entire towns are wiped from the face of the Empire. It is small wonder that many of these dispossessed folk go mad from the hopelessness and horror of their situation. To many, the wretched state of the world is seen as proof that its doom is at hand and only by bloody penitence and self-flagellation can it be saved. Such unfortunates flock to hear the despairing pronouncements of lunatic doomsayers, and these bands of Flagellants roam the Empire at will, spreading their gospel of desolation before them.

When war threatens, bands of crazed Flagellants instinctively gravitate towards battlefields, appearing unannounced and charging headlong towards the enemy without fear or hesitation. Flagellants fight in a crazed frenzy, driven insane by the horrors the world has inflicted upon them and desperate for their pain to end. Heedless of danger and injury, they will fight until each and every one of them is dead, thus vindicating their belief that the end is indeed nigh...

	M	WS	BS	S	T	W	I	A	Ld
Flagellant	4	2	2	3	3	1	3	1	10
Prophet of Doom	4	2	2	3	3	1	3	2	10

Special Rules
Unbreakable.

Crazed!: Flagellants are subject to the rules for Frenzy. Such is their insanity that they will never lose this, even if beaten in close combat.

The End is Nigh!: For some Flagellants, the risk of death in battle is not certain enough. Such martyrs hurl themselves to their death, leaping onto the weapons of their enemies or otherwise sacrificing themselves in as messy a way as possible. At the start of each round of close combat (their own and the enemy's), before any blows are struck, declare if the unit is going to sacrifice some martyrs or not. If you decide to go for it, roll a D3 to see how many Flagellants grandly sacrifice themselves. These models are removed in the same manner as combat casualties, except that they do not affect the number of Flagellants that can fight that phase and do not count as wounds suffered for the combat resolution score. Each martyr's death drives the Warband deeper into their madness and has the game effects listed below. These effects last until the end of that close combat phase and are cumulative, so if three martyrs are sacrificed, all three effects apply!

Number of Martyrs	Effect
1	The Flagellants Hate all enemies.
2	The Flagellants may re-roll failed rolls to wound.
3	Add +1 to the Flagellants' combat resolution score at the end of the close combat.

THE EMPEROR KARL FRANZ

The Emperor Karl Franz is said to be the greatest statesman the Old World has ever seen. He is acclaimed as a patron of arts and science, as a military innovator and as a valiant general. Thanks to his continual efforts, the Empire has flourished during his reign like never before: the Imperial Engineers School has grown, the Colleges of Magic have thrived and his armies have marched from victory to victory. The Emperor frequently takes personal command of his soldiers, wielding Ghal Maraz, the fabled hammer given to Sigmar by Kurgan Ironbeard over two thousand years ago.

In the years since his election, the Emperor has earned a magnificent record of victories and conquest. It was Karl Franz who led the charge of the Reiksguard that finally broke the Bretonnian Knights at the Battle of Norduin. On the Field of Blood, it was the Emperor's courage that steadied the Imperial line against the charges of a bloodthirsty Orc army. Against the Chaos horde of Morkhal-hai the Savage, the Emperor led his Greatswords into the very heart of the marauder army, where he crushed the enemy warlord's skull with Ghal Maraz.

Emperor Karl Franz often rides to battle on the back of Deathclaw, the Griffon he has raised from a hatchling. A powerful bond exists between the beast and its master, one forged in countless battles and many years of adventure. During the Battle of Blood Keep, Deathclaw stood over the wounded Emperor for three hours, slaying any who came near until the Reiksguard could hack a path to their fallen lord. Though it took the Emperor many months to recover, it is only thanks to the devotion of Deathclaw that he lived to fight another day.

Karl Franz is the best general the Empire army can field, and so it should be, as he is the Emperor! He can not only wield Ghal Maraz but also has access to various monstrous steeds. Most importantly, he is the only character in the Empire army with a Leadership of 10, and everyone within 18" can use it!

	M	WS	BS	S	T	W	I	A	Ld
Karl Franz	4	6	5	4	4	3	6	4	10
Deathclaw	6	6	–	5	5	4	5	4	8
The Imperial Dragon	6	6	–	6	6	6	3	5	8
Imperial Pegasus	8	3	–	4	4	3	4	2	6
Warhorse	8	3	–	3	3	1	3	1	5

Equipment

The Emperor wears full plate armour, the Silver Seal and is armed with either the Reikland's Runefang (see page 66) or the mighty Ghal Maraz.

Ghal Maraz: Meaning Skull-splitter in the Dwarf tongue, Ghal Maraz is the legendary hammer wielded by Sigmar himself when the Empire was forged over two and a half millennia ago. Any hits caused by the Hammer of Sigmar wound automatically and no armour saves are allowed. Each unsaved wound becomes D3 wounds.

The Silver Seal: The Warrior Mage Fredrik von Tarnus crafted this artefact for Magnus the Pious following the Great War Against Chaos. The Silver Seal wards away harmful blows and even disrupts hostile magic spells directed against the Emperor. It confers a 4+ ward save and magic resistance (3) upon the Emperor.

Special Rules

Leader of Men: The presence and unflinching courage of the Emperor greatly raises the morale of his soldiers, inspiring even the humblest of fighters to mighty acts of determined heroism. The Emperor and any unit he joins are immune to Psychology. In addition, the Emperor's Leadership can be used by friendly units in a range of 18" (instead of the 12" range for normal generals).

Deathclaw: Many years of war and adventure have developed an unbreakable bond between the Emperor and his beloved Griffon that transcends rider and mount. Deathclaw will automatically pass the Leadership test he needs to take if Karl Franz is slain. In addition, Deathclaw will Hate the character/unit that kills Karl Franz for the remainder of the game.

THE EMPEROR'S CAPITAL

The city of Altdorf is often called the capital of the Empire, though this is actually a misnomer, since Sigmar's realm has no fixed capital city as such. Since the Emperor is chosen from amongst the Elector Counts, the capital is wherever the current Emperor has his court. As such, the Empire's capital has changed many times over the centuries. With the election of Mandred Ratslayer following the Skaven wars, the Imperial court moved from Altdorf to Middenheim. After Mandred's death, numerous claimants vied for superiority and there were several 'capitals' in the anarchy of the Time of Three Emperors. The ascension of Magnus the Pious, the so-called Griffon Emperor, ended this division and the Imperial court came to Nuln. With the election of the Reikland Princes following the Marienburg scandal, the Imperial court once again took up residence in Altdorf. Many people (not least the Prince of Altdorf) view Altdorf as the first city of the Empire anyway, since it is built on the site of the Unberogen settlement of Reikdorf, the birthplace of Sigmar.

KURT HELBORG

Kurt Helborg is the Grand Marshal of the Reiksguard Knights and one of Emperor Karl Franz's most trusted military commanders. Tall and strong, he is the very image of a heroic Knight, his armour polished to a mirror sheen and his sword arm as strong as his courage is unbending. Captain of the Reiksguard, Helborg leads one of the Empire's most deadly warrior Orders, riding into battle atop a massive grey gelding said to have been sired by the finest stud in the Emperor's stables.

Helborg is reputed to be the greatest swordsman in the Old World, though this is a mantle hotly contested by the Emperor's Champion, Ludwig Schwarzhelm. The two warriors regularly compete on the field of battle to finally answer the question of who is the mightiest warrior of the Empire. So far, honours are roughly even, though Kurt Helborg is slightly ahead, much to Schwarzhelm's chagrin…

As the Reiksmarshal, Kurt Helborg is commander of all the Empire's armed forces, second only to the Emperor himself. As such, he has spent most of his life in battle, and is one of the most experienced generals in the Old World. Kurt Helborg has led the Reiksguard and Imperial armies in wars fought all across the Old World, from the dark forests of the Empire and icy wastes of Kislev to the blazing deserts of Araby.

As a general, he is virtually without peer, leading entire armies of Knights in thunderous charges of gleaming plate armour and glittering lance points. As a mighty warrior he fights where the combat is thickest, his Runefang cleaving the foe without mercy.

Kurt Helborg is a superb warrior, with a Weapon Skill on par with that of powerful Lord characters of other races. Not only that, but at the head of a force of Knightly Orders he strikes a hammer blow against enemy units.

	M	WS	BS	S	T	W	I	A	Ld
Kurt Helborg	4	7	3	4	4	3	6	4	9
Warhorse	8	3	–	3	3	1	3	1	5

Equipment
Kurt Helborg carries the Solland Runefang and wears full plate armour. He also wears the Laurels of Victory (see pages 66 and 69).

Mount: Kurt Helborg rides a barded Warhorse.

Special Rules
The Emperor's Chosen: The Reiksguard swear oaths to fight to the death in defence of the Emperor and no Knight would dare dishonour the order by failing to live up to this. Any unit of Reiksguard Knights led by Kurt Helborg is Stubborn as well as Immune to Psychology.

LUDWIG SCHWARZHELM

Ludwig Schwarzhelm is the champion of Karl Franz and the bearer of the Emperor's personal standard. Ludwig is a towering figure of a man renowned for his mighty physique, stern expression and deadly sword arm. Said to have never smiled in his life, this reputation as an uncompromising, incorruptible warrior is one Ludwig has cultivated over the years he has spent as the Emperor's Champion. His role is to uphold the Emperor's justice during trials of combat, which are the right of high-ranking nobles accused of disobeying the Emperor. Such is Ludwig's skill, many a noble so accused has pleaded guilty before a sword has even been lifted.

In addition to his formidable skills as a swordsman, Ludwig also acts as a potent reminder of the Emperor's authority, travelling to various provincial capitals to ensure that Imperial edicts are being obeyed. Ludwig's Sword of Justice has tasted the blood of many an Empire noble after an unannounced visit from the stern faced champion has revealed them to be little more than robber barons. The arrival of Ludwig Schwarzhelm at the gates of an Elector Count's castle is greeted with some trepidation, even amongst those staunchly loyal to the Emperor, for Schwarzhelm is notoriously inflexible and critical of those he perceives as lacking strong moral fibre and faith. On one occasion, Ludwig was forced to fight for his life after unmasking a Chaos cult at the heart of the von Rauken family of Ostland, but as dawn broke the following morning, it was the Emperor's Champion who marched alone from the castle, his armour battered and his sword bloodied.

When the Emperor travels through his lands, it is with the unsmiling Schwarzhelm beside him, and Karl Franz's diplomatic words are backed up by the threat of his champion's blade. In battle, Ludwig takes on the role of bodyguard and he has saved the Emperor's life on numerous occasions.

As Battle Standard Bearers go, Ludwig Schwarzhelm has some considerable advantages. Not only does he carry the Emperor's Standard to bolster surrounding units in combat, he also carries a magic weapon in the form of the Sword of Justice, a combination other Battle Standard Bearers cannot use.

	M	WS	BS	S	T	W	I	A	Ld
Ludwig Schwarzhelm	4	6	5	4	4	2	5	3	8
Warhorse	8	3	–	3	3	1	3	1	5

Equipment
Ludwig carries the Sword of Justice (see page 67) and wears full plate armour. Ludwig also bears the Emperor's Standard.

Mount: Ludwig rides a barded Warhorse.

The Emperor's Standard: This is the army's Battle Standard. In addition, in all combats with at least one friendly unit within 12" of the Emperor's Standard the friendly side receives an extra +1 to their total combat resolution (including the one involving Ludwig, which consequently receives a +2 bonus).

Special Rules
Killing Blow: Over his many trials by combat, Ludwig has perfected the art of killing quickly and cleanly. He has the Killing Blow special rule.

Bodyguard: The Emperor's safety is paramount to Ludwig and if the Emperor is in the same unit as Ludwig and fails a "Look Out, Sir!" roll, Ludwig takes the hit instead.

GRAND THEOGONIST VOLKMAR

Volkmar the Grim, Grand Theogonist of the Cult of Sigmar, is one of the most powerful Men in the Empire. Before the invasion of Archaon the Everchosen, Volkmar had been the sternest adherent of Sigmar's teachings, but malicious rumour-mongers cast doubts upon his devotion to the ideals of the Empire's warrior god. For days at a time he would lock himself in the secret repository of the tomes of forbidden lore, in search of an answer to the dark menace gathering in the far north.

Convinced only he could save the Empire, the fiery Volkmar marched north at the head of an army of Flagellants and Talabecland state troops to do battle with Archaon over the barren tundra of the Troll Country. Though the Grand Theogonist and his warriors fought heroically, they could not defeat the power of Archaon, and Volkmar himself was cut down by the Everchosen's daemon sword. Rather than allow the Grand Theogonist to rest in peace, the Daemon Be'lakor dragged Volkmar's soul back to his ravaged flesh and chained him to a daemonic standard in undying torment. Volkmar's spirit was forged of steel and he fought the malign influence of Chaos with every fibre of his being. During the Siege of Middenheim, Volkmar tore free from his hellish bondage and smote the Daemons with the enchanted chains that had once held him.

With Volkmar's return, clamouring voices cried for his reinstatement as Grand Theogonist, while supporters of his successor, Johann Esmer, branded him tainted by Chaos. Fearing a schism that could tear the Cult of Sigmar apart, the Arch Lectors despatched armed Men to 'persuade' Esmer that it would be better for all concerned if he were to step aside for Volkmar. Fearing for his life, Esmer fled to the city of Marienburg and Volkmar was swiftly ordained as Grand Theogonist once more.

As the most powerful Warrior Priest in the Empire, Volkmar the Grim is a potent addition to any army. Atop the War Altar of Sigmar he can crush enemies on the charge, while units around him fight with even greater effectiveness. On top of this, his prayers take great effort for your opponent to dispel.

	M	WS	BS	S	T	W	I	A	Ld
Grand Theogonist	4	5	3	4	4	3	4	2	9
The War Altar	–	–	–	5	5	5	–	–	–
Warhorse	8	3	–	3	–	–	3	1	5

Equipment
Sigmarite War Altar (see page 53), The Jade Griffon, the Staff of Command, the Horn of Sigismund.

The Jade Griffon: This talisman is carved from a huge piece of enchanted jade said to have been blessed by Magnus the Pious himself. The Jade Griffon hangs upon the Grand Theogonist's chest, glowing with a green inner light and draws its healing magic from the War Altar. While atop the War Altar, the Grand Theogonist benefits from a 5+ regeneration save.

The Staff of Command: The Grand Theogonist's badge of office, the staff draws power from the War Altar and channels it into the Grand Theogonist, adding +2 to his Strength. If the War Altar is destroyed then all bonuses are lost and the staff will count as a hand weapon.

The Horn of Sigismund: The Emperor Sigismund was given this enchanted horn by the Dwarfs after the Battle of Grimgrill Dale. After the death of Sigismund, the horn passed into the keeping of the Temple of Sigmar. It has remained in the temple ever since, and is blown three times on the anniversary of Sigismund's death. During the turn when they charge into combat, Volkmar and the War Altar cause Terror (from the moment it is found to be in charge range to the end of that turn), as Volkmar blows the horn.

Special Rules

Grand Theogonist: All the rules that apply to an Arch Lector (see page 52) apply to the Theogonist, except that his prayers are at power level 5.

Aura of Righteousness: So long as the War Altar is on the table, all Empire units within 12" of the altar benefit from the Grand Theogonist's Righteous Fury special rule.

Frenzy: So terrible was Volkmar's ordeal at the hands of the Daemon Be'lakor that his mind has been left bitter and twisted. Volkmar is subject to Frenzy.

SIGMAR'S HEIRS

As saviour and founder of the Empire, Sigmar is often considered to be symbolic of the entire realm. As such, the priesthood of Sigmar has a long-founded and enduring bond with the state and Imperial family, something many worshippers deplore as an unwelcome imposition upon their personal god. As a result many sects have grown up that worship Sigmar in their own way and, of all the gods, Sigmar inspires by far the most theosophical discussion and variation of belief and practice. In addition to the principal Holy Temple of Sigmar there are a great many splinter groups and several branches of Sigmarite theology. As dark times engulf the Empire once again, these differences of theology have given rise to a score of bizzare beliefs, birthing cults of mendicants, raving stylites, isolationist hermits, violent iconoclasts and wandering bands of apocalyptic flagellants. Each preaches a warped, self-sacrificing version of Sigmar's vision.

LUTHOR HUSS

Luthor Huss is a renegade Warrior Priest who travels throughout the Empire preaching the word of Sigmar and bringing death to followers of evil. Sent to Altdorf at an early age on a holy mission, Luthor was dismayed to see that many of the Priests of Sigmar were clergymen more concerned with politics than the holy mission bestowed upon them by Sigmar: the fight against Chaos.

With all the fervour of his burning faith, Luthor stood up in the cathedral of Sigmar and denounced the Lectors in the Council with hard words of reproach. Needless to say, Luthor was commanded to apologise by his superiors in the Order. Luthor was given three days to pray and consider the magnitude of what he had said, and at the end of this time, he was brought before the Arch Lectors to present his apology. Luthor was unrepentant. Furthermore, he renounced his position within the cult and took up his hammer as he left the cathedral to calls for his excommunication or death. From that day onwards, Luthor preached against corruption and roused the faithful to seek the will of Sigmar without the mediation of the clergy.

Luthor became the nightmare of every corrupt priest, the scourge of the unfaithful and the bane of those who consorted with the Dark Gods. Whispered rumours circulated that he was responsible for the deaths of several priests in Altdorf suspected of embezzling money from the collection plates. Tales of such grisly justice meted out at his hands drove the Arch Lectors of the cult of Sigmar to once again demand Luthor's excommunication. However Grand Theogonist Volkmar steadfastly refused to take such

drastic measures, prompting many to believe that the old man knew something of Luthor's ultimate destiny.

A portion of that destiny emerged following the defeat of Volkmar's army by Archaon in the northern wastes. In the midst of the Empire's despair, Luthor travelled the length and breadth of the land searching for signs and omens of Sigmar's return. Following incredible tales of a blacksmith's son, he travelled to the village of Lachenbad and discovered the young Valten, a boy in whom Luthor saw the power of Sigmar reborn. Luthor brought Valten to Altdorf and presented him to the Emperor, proclaiming him Sigmar reborn. Luthor had a great deal of support for his claims and could not easily be brushed aside. Karl Franz presented Valten with Ghal Maraz and dubbed him the Champion of Sigmar, marching alongside the young man to the final confrontation with Archaon before the walls of Middenheim.

Following the mysterious disappearance of Valten, Luthor Huss set off at the command of the Emperor into the wilds of the Empire. He began preaching that Sigmar would return once again in his people's darkest hour. Luthor appears most often whenever the forces of the Empire are facing evil and unholy enemies: Beastmen, Skaven or the Undead. All such abominations are blasphemies against Sigmar and must be destroyed by the faithful! Luthor fights with righteous fury beside the soldiers of the Empire, his warrior skills and fiery oratory an inspiration against such unholy foes.

Luthor Huss is a step above a normal Warrior Priest of Sigmar, and as a Hero makes a great general for smaller armies, or a good second-in-command for forces that can include one or more Lords.

	M	WS	BS	S	T	W	I	A	Ld
Luthor Huss	4	5	3	4	4	2	4	2	8
Warhorse	8	3	–	3	3	1	3	1	5

Equipment
Luthor Huss wields a two-handed hammer (great weapon) and wears heavy armour.

Mount: Luthor rides a barded Warhorse into battle.

Special Rules
Warrior Priest: All the rules that apply to Warrior Priests of Sigmar apply to Luthor Huss (see page 52).

The Chosen of Sigmar: The power of Sigmar surrounds Luthor in battle and protects him from evil. Luthor has a 4+ ward save.

Cause Fear: Such is Luthor's reputation as the scourge of the Empire's enemies that he causes Fear.

THE MARCH OF DOOM

Crazed zealots march throughout the Empire, bearing icons of doom before them and preaching that the end of the world is nigh. Upon reaching a town or village, they call its inhabitants to bear witness to their gruesome self-mortification. When a sufficient crowd has gathered, the Flagellants scour themselves with whips and barbed chains until their flesh is bloody, rejoicing and singing praise to Sigmar as they do so.

Amid the whipping and screaming, a prophet of doom shrieks of the grievous sins of Mankind and cries that only those who join their cavalcade of agony can save the world. Such is the force of passion and fervour of the prophet's oratory that many in the audience cast off their former lives and join the Flagellant band. In time, a great procession trudges from town to town, bearing their knotted scourges and chanting their melancholy dirges.

BALTHASAR GELT

Balthasar Gelt came to Altdorf from Marienburg, having bought passage on a merchant ship with gold that he had transmuted from lead ingots. He left the seaport for the Colleges of Magic before the effects wore off, and now rumours abound that the swindled sea captain has placed a rich bounty on Balthasar – though few would dare attempt to collect it.

The transmutation of vile metals into pure gold, the noblest metal of all, had always fascinated him and, driven by his obsession, Balthasar rose quickly through the ranks of the Gold Order. He spent many years experimenting on combining science with the Lore of Metal, his fierce intelligence and open-minded approach leading him to a greater understanding of this branch of magic than any other Wizard. Balthasar's research into new formulations of black powder even made him popular with the College of Engineers, an organisation that often dismisses magic as superstitious nonsense.

A freak explosion in the laboratory almost ended Balthasar's quest for knowledge, though some remembered the sea captain's bounty and believed it was no accident. From that day, Balthasar has only ever been seen swathed in shimmering, metallic robes and wearing a golden mask. Some say his entire skin turned to gold while others tell that he is horribly disfigured, though the truth of the matter is unknown. One thing is certain: the accident only furthered his will to succeed and increased his powers. After defeating Thyrus Gormann of the Bright Order in ritual duel, Balthasar became Supreme Patriarch, replacing the prominence of Fire with that of Metal. Since that day, the new Supreme Patriarch, riding a Pegasus and surrounded by a golden halo, has appeared on many battlefields where the Emperor's soldiers are fighting.

Quite simply the most powerful wizard in the Empire, Balthasar Gelt will dominate the magic phase!

	M	WS	BS	S	T	W	I	A	Ld
Balthasar Gelt	4	3	3	3	4	3	3	1	8
Imperial Pegasus	8	3	–	4	4	3	4	2	6

Equipment
Sword (hand weapon), Al-kahest, Staff of Volans, The Cloak of Molten Metal, Amulet of Sea Gold.

Mount: Balthasar rides a Pegasus into battle.

Al-kahest: In the shooting phase, Balthasar can throw a vial of highly acidic alchemical substances. The vials have a range of 6" and follow the rules for throwing weapons. If the vial hits, it will shatter, wounding any target on a 4+. No armour saving throws are allowed against these wounds. This counts as both a magical and a flaming attack.

Staff of Volans: This staff belonged to Volans, first Patriarch of the Colleges of Magic, who was taught by Teclis of Ulthuan during the Great War Against Chaos. The Staff of Volans gives +2 to the casting attempts made by Balthasar. In addition, it allows him to ignore the first miscast he suffers. In this case, the spell does not work, but Balthasar does not need to roll on the miscast table.

The Cloak of Molten Metal: This mystic robe creates a shimmering series of images of the Wizard and his mount, forever rotating in a dazzling whirlwind of iridescent colours, confusing the aim of anybody attacking them with a ranged weapon. The robe gives a 3+ ward save against any missile attack directed towards Balthasar and his mount.

Amulet of Sea Gold: An ancient Elven heirloom unearthed by Balthasar in the ruins of one of the abandoned colonies of the Elves on the Estalian coast. The amulet grants Balthasar magic resistance (1).

Special Rules
Alchemist Supreme. Balthasar is a level 4 Wizard and always uses spells from the Lore of Metal (see the Warhammer rulebook). Balthasar knows all six spells from the list, so there is no need to roll for spells before the battle.

IMPERER · REX · HONORIS KARL FRANZ

HEIRLOOMS OF MAGIC

In this section the common magic items are listed first (see page 122 of the Warhammer rulebook for a complete description). 'Empire only' magic items are also listed and these can only be used by models from this book. Any magic items chosen must be selected within the points limitations set by the army list section. All the rules on magic items presented in the Warhammer rulebook also apply to the 'Empire only' magic items.

Common Magic Items

Sword of Striking: . . . . **15 points**
Weapon; +1 to hit

Sword of Battle: . . . . **15 points**
Weapon; +1 Attack

Sword of Might: . . . . **15 points**
Weapon; +1 Strength

Biting Blade: . . . . **5 points**
Weapon; -1 armour save

Enchanted Shield: . . . . **15 points**
Armour; 5+ armour save

Talisman of Protection: . . . . **15 points**
Talisman; 6+ ward save

Dispel Scroll : . . . . **25 points**
Arcane; one use only; Automatically dispel an enemy spell.

Power Stone: . . . . **20 points**
Arcane; one use only; +2 dice to cast a spell

Staff of Sorcery: . . . . **35 points**
Arcane; +1 to dispel

War Banner: . . . . **25 points**
Banner; +1 combat resolution

Magic Weapons

Runefang (General of the Empire only) **100 points**
At the dawn of the Empire, a dozen magical blades were forged for Sigmar's twelve chieftains. Amongst the oldest and most treasured artefacts still surviving in the Empire, these Runefangs are synonymous with the status and authority of the Elector Counts. The Runefang that once belonged to the province of Solland is now wielded by Kurt Helborg, the Reiksmarshal. The remaining blade is kept in the Imperial vaults and occasionally presented to heroic Generals who are fighting in the service of the Empire.

All hits from a Runefang wound automatically and allow no armour saves.

The Mace of Helsturm   **60 points**
This mace was used in battle by the first Theogonist, Johann Helsturm. It is said that Helsturm's faith in Sigmar was strong enough to shatter the walls of a castle, and that his mace retains a portion of his holy might.

The bearer can forfeit all of his normal Attacks to make only one Attack. Roll to hit normally. If this one Attack hits, the hit is resolved at Strength 10 and causes D6 wounds.

Sword of Sigismund   **45 points**
This sword, wielded in the crusades by the Grand Master of the Knights Panther, once belonged to Emperor Sigismund and has been passed down through all the Princes of Altdorf since then.

The wielder of this sword strikes with +1 Strength and benefits from the 'always strikes first' special rule in close combat.

Sword of Fate   **40 points**
The blade of this enchanted weapon was forged beneath a spiteful moon and has been enchanted with bitter tears to be the undoing of one specific foe.

At the beginning of the battle, nominate one enemy character or monster. The sword counts as a magic sword with no particular bonuses against any other opponent, but attacks directed against the designated target will wound it on a 2+ and cause D3 wounds, with no armour saves allowed.

Sword of Power   **40 points**
Forged from the hardest star metal, the wielder of this weapon is bestowed with supernatural strength, his every blow is able to smash through the thickest of armour with ease.

The sword confers +2 Strength to all close combat attacks made by the character.

Sword of Righteous Steel   **30 points**
Swords made of the purest steel can be blessed by a priest of Sigmar to greatly enhance the fighting skills of their wielder. Each swift blow seeks out the enemy's vitals and is almost impossible to parry.

The wielder always hits any opponent on a 2+, regardless of relative Weapon Skills. This cannot be modified in any way.

Hammer of Judgement   25 points

This mighty hammer was said to have been carried into battle by Frederick the Bold, great-grandfather of Emperor Karl Franz. Its mighty strikes not only crush flesh and bone, but evil spirits are cast to ruin as well.

Models hit by this hammer must take a Toughness test for every hit suffered. If the test is failed, the hit wounds automatically and no armour save is allowed. If the test is passed, roll to wound and take armour saves as normal.

Dragon Bow   25 points

A relic from the ancient Elven colonies of the Old World, this wondrously crafted bow enables the wielder to outshoot the best archers in the Empire.

The Dragon Bow has a range of 36" and Strength 6. Any hits from this bow count as being from a magical weapon.

Sword of Justice   20 points

The Sword of Justice is an ancient weapon passed down from champion to champion through the reigns of successive Emperors. It is studded with ancient Dwarf runes of vengeance and retribution that bestow the power of unswerving accuracy and deadly retribution upon it.

The bearer can re-roll failed rolls to wound.

Wyrmslayer Sword   15 points

The blade of Ulfdar the Berserker, who fought alongside Sigmar at Black Fire Pass, the Wyrmslayer Sword has been the doom of many a monster that has menaced the Empire.

Hits from this sword wound any opponent on a roll of 4+ (unless the wielder's Strength would make this less). Armour saves apply as normal, modified by the Strength of the character, but large targets lose their armour save due to the scaly skin special rule against hits from this sword.

Magic Armour

The Gilded Armour   40 points

This golden suit of armour was a gift from the Elves of Ulthuan to Magnus the Pious after the Great War Against Chaos. It repels weapons with an invisible force.

Heavy armour. Models attacking the wearer in close combat must pass a Strength test before rolling to hit for every Attack directed at the target. If the test is failed, the Attack is lost. Special Attacks (like those of a Giant, impact hits and anything not included in the Attacks value on a model's profile) are not affected.

Dawn Armour   35 points

A Master Wizard of the Gold Order forged this suit of plate under the first rays of the sun. The enchantment concealed in the metal will repair any damage within an eyeblink.

Full plate armour (armour save 4+). The model can re-roll any failed armour save.

Armour of Tarnus   35 points

This armour was worn by the warrior wizard Frederick von Tarnus. Such was the power invested in the armour's forging that von Tarnus' own magic was unaffected by its protection.

Light armour. The Armour of Tarnus confers a 5+ ward save to the wearer. Wizards can wear this armour and cast spells.

Armour of Meteoric Iron   25 points

This suit of armour, long ago forged by the Dwarf smiths of Zhufbar, is today held in the Imperial Armoury at Altdorf. Only the greatest heroes of the Empire may don this magnificent suit of armour.

This armour gives the bearer a 1+ armour save that cannot be improved by any means.

Helm of the Ratslayer   25 points

The legendary helm of Count Mandred Ratslayer was crafted from the skull of the warlord who fell at the Battle of the Howling Hills. Such is its reputation amongst the rat-spawn that they dread to face its wearer.

This helm confers a 6+ armour save which can be combined with other equipment normally (including normal armour and a shield). In addition, the wearer causes Fear in all models in a Skaven army.

Shield of the Gorgon   25 points

The image on this shield represents the head of a Gorgon, a hideous monster said to dwell in the harsh deserts of Araby. Enemies try to avoid its gaze, for the eyes of a Gorgon are rumoured to turn living creatures to stone.

Shield. The wearer can force one model in base contact to lose one Attack. In the case of models with different Attacks (eg, mounted models) the wearer chooses which Attack is lost. Special Attacks (like those of a Giant, impact hits and anything not included in the Attacks value on a model's profile) are not affected.

Bronze Shield   20 points

A shield made of bronze can carry a powerful enchantment of protection, but only for a short time.

Shield. The bearer ignores the first hit in the battle from shooting or close combat.

Talismans

Shroud of Magnus   50 points

This ancient shroud was laid upon the body of Magnus the Pious after his death. On it one can still see the features of the Saviour of the Empire, his countenance as noble in death as it was in life.

This item gives the bearer a 5+ ward save and magic resistance (2).

Holy Relic   45 points

The most famous holy relic in the Empire is the icon of Sigmar carried by the Arch Lector of Nuln, a token which is said to grant the bearer great fortitude.

The Holy Relic gives its bearer a 4+ ward save.

Jade Amulet   40 points

The Grand Theogonist sometimes grants a shard of the Jade Griffon, his badge of office, as a reward for great services performed in the name of Sigmar.

The model may ignore the first wound it suffers.

The White Cloak   35 points

This cloak has been enchanted by Ar-Ulric, the High Priest of the Sect of Ulric, the god of winter and war. The magics of the cloak frost the air around the wearer, rendering him almost immune to even the hottest flame.

This item gives a 5+ ward save, which is increased to 2+ against Flaming Attacks.

The Crimson Amulet   20 points

Originally possessed by a tribal chieftain at the time of Sigmar, legends say that the bearer of this rough-hewn pendant is capable of performing exceptional displays of strength and agility.

This item gives a 6+ ward save. The wearer automatically passes any characteristic tests he has to take (except Leadership tests).

Sigil of Sigmar   15 points

The symbol of Sigmar may take many forms such as a twin-tailed comet, hammer, crown or griffon. Regardless of form, each has the power to protect the wearer from the ravages of hostile magics.

The Sigil of Sigmar confers magic resistance (1).

Arcane Items

Seal of Destruction   45 points

Seven of these seals were originally crafted under Elven tutelage, each capable of draining the knowledge of a spell from the mind of an enemy Wizard.

One use only. The seal has the same effect as a Dispel Scroll. In addition, roll a D6. On a result of 4+ the spell is removed from the caster's mind and he can no longer cast it. Spells cast from a bound item will only be removed on the result of a 6.

Grey Wand   40 points

The Archmage Ptolos of the Grey College won this wand at the Battle of Blood Keep.

Gives +1 to the casting attempts made by the Wizard.

Rod of Power   30 points

The Rod of Power absorbs magical energy that its bearer can use to boost his own spells.

At the end of each magic phase (yours and enemy's), you can save up to three unused power/dispel dice from the pool and store them in the rod. At the beginning of each successive magic phase (yours and enemy's), roll a dice. If the result is equal or higher to the number of dice stored, add them to the power/dispel dice pool, if the result is lower than the number of dice stored, they are lost.

Luckstone   25 points

Charged with divinatory power, these stones are very useful when a Wizard is manipulating the delicate balance of the Winds of Magic.

One use only. Once per battle, the bearer can re-roll all of the dice rolled to cast or dispel a spell. This can effectively cancel a miscast result, and cause irresistible force or a miscast.

Crystal Ball   15 points

Nothing is hidden from the inquisitive gaze of Wizards using this powerful scrying device.

The enemy must always reveal all the 'secrets' involving all units that are within 24" of the Wizard at any time. This includes which magic items are in the unit and who is carrying them, the presence of disguised, hidden or otherwise 'invisible' models and everything else that the player is not normally obliged to disclose to his opponent.

Wizard's Staff   10 points

Throughout the Empire, many Wizards carry a staff as a mark of their office and as an aid in the focussing and control of sorcerous powers.

The Wizard's Staff allows the bearer to use one more dice than he is normally allowed to when casting a spell (eg, a Wizard that can normally use up to two dice to cast spells will be able to use up to three dice).

Enchanted Items

Laurels of Victory   55 points

The most celebrated heroes of the Empire are decorated with golden laurels enchanted by the Imperial Wizards. The magic within this symbol of victory magnifies the bearer's presence and stature in the eyes of his enemy to the point that few foes have courage enough to stand before his wrath.

Each wound caused by a model wearing the Laurels of Victory (but not those caused by his mount) will count as 2 Wounds when working out combat resolution. Note that you do not actually cause double wounds on your victim!

Rod of Command   50 points

A gift from the Teclis to Magnus the Pious, the Rod of Command has the power to instil courage even in the face of the most dire of perils. When the battle seems lost, the bearer can summon the powers of the rod to turn a certain rout into steadfast resistance.

One use only. Whenever the character (and the unit he is with) have to take a Break test, instead of rolling the dice, the player can declare he is using this item. If the player decides to do so, the character (and his unit) automatically roll double 1s (Insane Courage!) for the test, automatically passing it regardless of modifiers. This item cannot be used by a character in a turn he refused a challenge or if he is hiding at the back of the unit (nobody would pay heed to such a coward!).

Aldred's Casket of Sorcery   35 points

The casket has the power to entrap and contain the power of magic forever, as Aldred unwittingly discovered when he opened it in the presence of the Supreme Patriarch of the Colleges of Magic. Aldred was not seen thereafter.

Bound Spell: Power Level variable. At the end of each of his movement phases, the bearer may remove and capture one randomly determined spell from an enemy Wizard within 12" of him on a roll of 4+. The bearer can then cast the captured spell in any of his own following magic phases by releasing it from the casket just like from a bound item, whereupon the spell is then removed from the game. Any number of spells may be captured by the casket, and the bearer can cast each one once, either over several magic phases or all at the same time if he prefers. The power level of the spell cast by the casket will be equivalent to the normal casting value of the spell.

The Silver Horn   35 points

This elegant hunting horn contains a potent spell. Friends who hear its note are filled with courage.

Bound Spell: Power Level 5. If successfully cast, all fleeing friendly units on the battlefield will rally immediately, regardless of the number of models left.

The Orb of Thunder   30 points

The Orb of Thunder contains a powerful spell that wreaks turmoil in the air, summoning dark thunderclouds and mighty winds.

Bound Spell: Power Level 4. Remains in play. When the Orb of Thunder spell is in play, flying creatures on the battlefield cannot fly and must move on the ground at their normal Movement rate.

Doomfire Ring   30 points

The Doomfire Ring, made of dark iron and flame rubies, contains a powerful spell that allows its master to cast fire upon his enemies.

Bound Spell: Power Level 3. The Doomfire Ring casts the Burning Head spell from the Lore of Fire (see the Warhammer rulebook).

Van Horstmann's Speculum   30 points

This tiny mirror hangs around the wearer's neck and has been enchanted with the ability to reflect the fighting qualities of an enemy back upon himself.

When the wearer fights a challenge he can 'swap' his base Weapon Skill, Strength, Toughness, Initiative and Attacks values with those of his enemy. He can choose not to use the mirror, but if he does he must swap all these characteristics for the duration of the challenge. So, the wearer fights with his enemy's WS, S, T, I and A whilst his enemy fights with the wearer's WS, S, T, I and A.

Icon of Magnus   25 points

The presence of this revered relic among their ranks fills the soldiers with faith and strengthens their resolve. They will fight on even against the most dreadful of enemies.

The character and the unit he is with are immune to Fear. When faced with an enemy that causes Terror, the character and the unit he is with only suffer Fear, not Terror.

Ring of Volans   20 points

Volans was the greatest of the pupils of Teclis, the founder of the Colleges of Magic. His ring still resonates with the magical power its master once commanded.

One use only. Bound Spell: Power Level variable. Choose any one of the eight magic lores in the Warhammer rulebook and randomly select one spell from that lore to be bound within the Ring of Volans. The power level of the spell cast by the ring will be equivalent to the normal casting value of the spell.

Magic Standards

Imperial Banner   100 points
Woven upon Elven silks and embroidered with the commandments of Sigmar, the standard which carries the ruling Emperor's blazon fills nearby troops with a supreme sense of duty and pride.

All units with at least one model within 12" of the Imperial Banner can re-roll any failed Terror, Fear, Panic or Rally test as well as tests to avoid pursuing a fleeing enemy.

Banner of Sigismund   60 points
Emperor Sigismund, the hero of the Siege of Altdorf, held this banner aloft from the roof of his palace. It survived the siege and was never touched by the Orcish invaders – which is more than can be said for Sigismund.

The standard bearer and all models in his unit are Stubborn. Note that this bonus is also conferred to other characters within the unit.

Griffon Standard   55 points
In the folktales of the Empire, the Griffon is a stalwart and stubborn beast that refuses to be bested in combat, no matter how outmatched it may be. In honour of this, a unit flying the Griffon Standard resolutely stands its ground, and few foes can break them.

A unit joined by a Battle Standard Bearer carrying the Griffon Standard counts double its rank bonus when it comes to working out combat results. If the unit is in two ranks it receives +2, in three ranks +4, and in four ranks (the maximum bonus) +6. The unit will never pursue a fleeing enemy, but will always hold its ground, even if affected by a special rule that means it must normally do so.

Banner of the Daemonslayer   50 points
(Knightly Orders only)
This banner was carried at the Battle of Middenheim, and was dipped in the blood of a mighty Daemon Prince.

During the turn when it charges into combat, the unit causes Fear (from the moment it is found to be in charge range to the end of that turn).

Banner of Valour   30 points
Held high by Solland's Greatswords in their renowned last stand against Orc invaders, this banner is a symbol of sacrifice and ultimate devotion to duty.

The unit is Immune to Panic.

Standard of Arcane Warding   30 points
This magic banner absorbs the power of hostile spells and discharges it into the air.

This banner confers magic resistance (2) on the unit that carries it.

Steel Standard (Knightly Orders only)   20 points
Enchanted by the wizards of the Golden Order, this standard affects the heavy metal barding of Knights' warhorses, making it lighter.

The unit can add D3" to its charge move. If the charge is failed, the unit will move forward 7" as normal.

Banner of Duty   10 points
This banner shines with a soothing light that reaches into the hearts of warriors in despair, filling them with courage and renewing their will to fight on.

The unit can re-roll any failed Rally test.

THE EMPIRE ARMY LIST

This army list enables you to turn your Citadel miniatures collection into an army ready for a tabletop battle. As described in the Warhammer rulebook, the army list is divided into four sections: Characters (including Lords and Heroes), Core Units, Special Units and Rare Units.

Choosing an Army

Every miniature in the Warhammer range has a points cost that reflects how effective it is on the battlefield. For example, a lowly Halberdier costs just 5 points, while a mighty Templar Grand Master costs 145 points!

Both players choose armies to the same agreed points total. You can spend less and will probably find it impossible to use up every last point. Most '2,000 point' armies, for example, will be something like 1,998 or 1,999 points.

To form your miniatures into an army, look up the relevant army list entry for the first troop type. This tells you the points cost to add each unit of models to your army and any options or upgrades the unit may have. Then select your next unit, calculate its points and so on until you reach the agreed points total. In addition to the points, there are a few other rules that govern which units you can include in your army, as detailed under Choosing Characters and Choosing Troops.

Army List Entries

Profiles. The characteristic profiles for the model(s) in each unit are provided as a reminder. Where several profiles are required, these are also given even if they are optional.

Unit Size. Each troop entry specifies the minimum size for each unit, which is the smallest number of models needed to form that unit. In some cases units also have a maximum size.

Equipment. Each entry lists the standard weapons and armour for that unit type. The cost of these items is included in the basic points value. Additional or optional weapons and armour cost extra and are covered in the Options section of the unit entry.

Special Rules. Many troops have special rules that are fully described earlier in this book. The names of these rules are listed as a reminder.

Options. Many entries list different weapon, armour and equipment options, along with any additional points cost for giving them to the unit. This includes magic items and other upgrades for characters. It may also include the option to upgrade a unit member to a champion, standard bearer or musician.

Choosing Characters

Characters are divided into two categories: Lords and Heroes. The maximum number of characters an army can include is shown on the chart below. Of these, only a certain number can be Lords.

Army Points Value	Max. Total Characters	Max. Lords	Max. Heroes
Less than 2,000	3	0	3
2,000 or more	4	1	4
3,000 or more	6	2	6
4,000 or more	8	3	8
Each +1,000	+2	+1	+2

An army must always include at least one character to act as the general. If you include more than one character, then the one with the highest Leadership value is the general. When one or more characters have the same (and highest) Leadership, choose one to be the general at the start of the battle. Make sure that your opponent knows which character is your general when you deploy your army.

Choosing Troops

The number of each type of unit allowed depends on the army's points value.

Army Points Value	Core Units	Special Units	Rare Units
Less than 2,000	2+	0-3	0-1
2,000 or more	3+	0-4	0-2
3,000 or more	4+	0-5	0-3
4,000 or more	5+	0-6	0-4
Each +1,000	+1 minimum	+0-1	+0-1

LORDS

THE EMPEROR KARL FRANZ

Points: 350

	M	WS	BS	S	T	W	I	A	Ld
Karl Franz	4	6	5	4	4	3	6	4	10
Deathclaw	6	6	–	5	5	4	5	4	8
The Imperial Dragon	6	6	–	6	6	6	3	5	8
Imperial Pegasus	8	3	–	4	4	3	4	2	6
Warhorse	8	3	–	3	3	1	3	1	5

Your army can only include one Karl Franz model.

EQUIPMENT: Runefang, The Silver Seal, full plate armour.

SPECIAL RULES:
Leader of Men.

OPTIONS:
• May replace his Runefang with Ghal Maraz (+30 pts).

• May ride Deathclaw the Griffon (+225 pts), the Imperial Dragon (+320 pts), an Imperial Pegasus (+50 pts) or a barded Warhorse (+21 pts).

ARMY ORGANISATION:
If your army is led by Karl Franz, one unit of State Troops can have a magic banner worth up to 50 points.

KURT HELBORG

Points: 325

	M	WS	BS	S	T	W	I	A	Ld
Kurt Helborg	4	7	3	4	4	3	6	4	9
Warhorse	8	3	–	3	3	1	3	1	5

Your army can only include one Kurt Helborg model.

MOUNT: Barded Warhorse.

EQUIPMENT: Runefang, full plate armour, Laurels of Victory.

SPECIAL RULES:
The Emperor's Chosen.

ARMY ORGANISATION:
You may only field Kurt Helborg if your army contains a unit of Reiksguard Knights.

GRAND THEOGONIST VOLKMAR

Points: 360

	M	WS	BS	S	T	W	I	A	Ld
Grand Theogonist	4	5	3	4	4	3	4	2	9
The War Altar	–	–	–	5	5	5	–	–	–
Warhorse	8	3	–	3	–	–	3	1	5

Your army can only include one Volkmar model.

EQUIPMENT: The Jade Griffon, the Staff of Command and the Horn of Sigismund.

SPECIAL RULES:
Grand Theogonist; Aura of Righteousness; Frenzy.

BALTHASAR GELT

Points: 400

	M	WS	BS	S	T	W	I	A	Ld
Balthasar Gelt	4	3	3	3	4	3	3	1	8
Imperial Pegasus	8	3	–	4	4	3	4	2	6

Your army can only include one Balthasar Gelt model.

MAGIC: Balthasar Gelt is a level 4 Wizard. He knows all the spells from the Lore of Metal.

MOUNT: Imperial Pegasus

EQUIPMENT: Sword (hand weapon), Al-kahest, Staff of Volans, The Cloak of Molten Metal, Amulet of Sea Gold.

SPECIAL RULES:
Alchemist Supreme.

LORDS

GENERAL OF THE EMPIRE

Points: 80

	M	WS	BS	S	T	W	I	A	Ld
General of the Empire	4	5	5	4	4	3	5	3	9
Griffon	6	5	–	5	5	4	5	4	7
Imperial Pegasus	8	3	–	4	4	3	4	2	6
Warhorse	8	3	–	3	3	1	3	1	5

EQUIPMENT: Hand weapon.

ARMY ORGANISATION:

Ancestral Heirloom. If your army is led by a General of the Empire, one unit of State Troops can have a magic banner worth up to 50 points.

OPTIONS:

- May have a great weapon (+6 pts), an additional hand weapon (+6 pts) and/or a pistol (+9 pts).

- May have a longbow (+10 pts) and/or a handgun (+10 pts).

- May wear light armour (+3 pts), heavy armour (+6 pts) or full plate armour (+12 pts). May also carry a shield (+3 pts).

- May ride either a Warhorse (+15 pts), which can have barding (+6 pts), an Imperial Pegasus (+50 pts) or a Griffon (+200 pts). If mounted, he may have a lance (+6 pts).

- May choose up to 100 points of magic items chosen from the Common and Empire magic items lists.

TEMPLAR GRAND MASTER

Points: 145

	M	WS	BS	S	T	W	I	A	Ld
Grand Master	4	6	3	4	4	3	6	4	9
Warhorse	8	3	–	3	3	1	3	1	5

MOUNT: Barded Warhorse.

EQUIPMENT: Hand weapon, full plate armour and either a lance and a shield or a great weapon.

SPECIAL RULES:
Master of Battle.

OPTIONS:

- May choose up to 100 points of magic items chosen from the Common and Empire magic items lists.

ARMY ORGANISATION:

You may only field a Templar Grand Master if your army contains a unit of Knights of the same Order.

ARCH LECTOR OF SIGMAR

Points: 125

	M	WS	BS	S	T	W	I	A	Ld
Arch Lector	4	4	3	4	4	3	4	2	9
The War Altar	–	–	–	5	5	5	–	–	–
Warhorse	8	3	–	3	3	1	3	1	5

EQUIPMENT: Warhammer (hand weapon).

SPECIAL RULES:
Blessings of Sigmar; Righteous Fury; Prayers of Sigmar.

OPTIONS:

- May choose a two-handed hammer (great weapon, +6 pts) or a second warhammer if on foot (+6 pts).

- May wear either light armour (+3 pts) or heavy armour (+6 pts) and may also carry a shield (+3 pts).

- May ride a Warhorse (+15 pts), which may be barded (+6 pts).

- May ride upon the War Altar of Sigmar (+100 pts).

- May choose up to 100 points of magic items chosen from the Common and Empire magic items lists.

WIZARD LORD

Points: 175

	M	WS	BS	S	T	W	I	A	Ld
Wizard Lord	4	3	3	3	4	3	3	1	8
Imperial Pegasus	8	3	–	4	4	3	4	2	6
Warhorse	8	3	–	3	3	1	3	1	5

MAGIC: Level 3 Wizard. May choose from any one of the eight Lores of Magic described in the Warhammer rulebook.

EQUIPMENT: Hand weapon.

OPTIONS:

- May be upgraded to a level 4 Wizard for +35 points.

- May ride either a Warhorse (+15 pts), which can have barding (+6 pts), or an Imperial Pegasus (+50 pts).

- May choose up to 100 points of magic items chosen from the Common and Empire magic items lists.

HEROES

 ## LUDWIG SCHWARZHELM

Points: 220

	M	WS	BS	S	T	W	I	A	Ld
Ludwig Schwarzhelm	4	6	5	4	4	2	5	3	8
Warhorse	8	3	–	3	3	1	3	1	5

Your army can only include one Ludwig model.

MOUNT: Barded Warhorse.

EQUIPMENT: Sword of Justice, full plate armour.

SPECIAL RULES:
The Emperor's Standard; Killing Blow; Bodyguard.

ARMY ORGANISATION:
If you field Ludwig Schwarzhelm, you cannot take a Captain of the Empire carrying the battle standard.

 ## LUTHOR HUSS

Points: 180

	M	WS	BS	S	T	W	I	A	Ld
Luthor Huss	4	5	3	4	4	2	4	2	8
Warhorse	8	3	–	3	3	1	3	1	5

Your army can only include one Luthor Huss model.

MOUNT: Barded Warhorse.

EQUIPMENT: Two-handed warhammer (great weapon), heavy armour.

SPECIAL RULES:
Warrior Priest; Cause Fear; Chosen of Sigmar.

HEROES

CAPTAIN OF THE EMPIRE

Points: 50

	M	WS	BS	S	T	W	I	A	Ld
Captain of the Empire	4	5	5	4	4	2	5	3	8
Imperial Pegasus	8	3	–	4	4	3	4	2	6
Warhorse	8	3	–	3	3	1	3	1	5

EQUIPMENT: Hand weapon.

OPTIONS:

- May have a great weapon (+4 pts), a halberd (+4 pts), an additional hand weapon (+4 pts) and/or a pistol (+6 pts).

- May also have either a longbow (+10 pts) or a handgun (+10 pts).

- May wear either light armour (+2 pts), heavy armour (+4 pts), or full plate armour (+8 pts), and may also carry a shield (+2 pts).

- May ride either a Warhorse (+10 pts), which can have barding (+4 pts), or an Imperial Pegasus (+50 pts). If mounted, he may choose a lance (+4 pts),

- May choose up to 50 points of magic items chosen from the Common and Empire magic items lists.

Battle Standard Bearer: One Captain in the army can carry the battle standard for +25 points. The battle standard bearer cannot be the army's general, even if he has the highest Leadership value. The battle standard bearer cannot choose any non-magical equipment except for light, heavy or full plate armour and/or barding for his steed. He cannot ride an Imperial Pegasus. The battle standard bearer can have any magic banner (no points limit), but if he carries a magic banner, he cannot carry any other magic item.

WARRIOR PRIEST

Points: 90

	M	WS	BS	S	T	W	I	A	Ld
Warrior Priest	4	4	3	4	4	2	4	2	8
Warhorse	8	3	–	3	3	1	3	1	5

EQUIPMENT: Warhammer (hand weapon).

SPECIAL RULES:
Blessings of Sigmar; Righteous Fury; Prayers of Sigmar.

OPTIONS:

- May have a two-handed hammer (great weapon, +4 pts) and/or a second warhammer if on foot (+4 pts).

- May wear either light armour (+2 pts) or heavy armour (+4 pts). May also carry a shield (+2 pts).

- May ride a Warhorse (+10 pts), which may be barded (+4 pts).

- May choose up to 50 points of magic items chosen from the Common and Empire magic items lists.

BATTLE WIZARD

Points: 65

	M	WS	BS	S	T	W	I	A	Ld
Battle Wizard	4	3	3	3	3	2	3	1	7
Warhorse	8	3	–	3	3	1	3	1	5

MAGIC: Level 1 Wizard. May choose from any one of the eight Lores of Magic described in the Warhammer rulebook.

EQUIPMENT: Hand weapon.

OPTIONS:

- May be upgraded to a Level 2 Wizard for +35 points.

- May ride a Warhorse (+10 pts), which may be barded (+4 pts).

- May choose up to 50 points of magic items chosen from the Common and Empire magic items lists.

MASTER ENGINEER

Points: 65

	M	WS	BS	S	T	W	I	A	Ld
Master Engineer	4	3	4	3	3	2	3	1	7
Warhorse	8	3	–	3	3	1	3	1	5

EQUIPMENT: Hand weapon.

SPECIAL RULES:
Master of Ballistics; Extra Crewman.

OPTIONS:

- May wear light armour (+2 pts).

- May ride either a Warhorse (+10 pts), which can have barding (+4 pts), or a mechanical steed (+25 pts).

- May have a repeater pistol (+10 pts), a Hochland long rifle (+20 pts), a grenade launching blunderbuss (+10 pts), a repeater handgun (+15 pts) and/or pigeon bombs (+25 pts).

CORE UNITS

HALBERDIERS

Points/model: 5

	M	WS	BS	S	T	W	I	A	Ld
Halberdier	4	3	3	3	3	1	3	1	7
Sergeant	4	3	3	3	3	1	3	2	7

UNIT SIZE: 10+

EQUIPMENT: Hand weapon, halberd, light armour.

SPECIAL RULES:
State Troops.

OPTIONS:
- Any unit may be equipped with shields for +1 pt/per model.
- Upgrade one Halberdier to a musician for +4 pts.
- Upgrade one Halberdier to a standard bearer for +8 pts.
- Promote one Halberdier to a Sergeant for +8 pts.

SPEARMEN

Points/model: 5

	M	WS	BS	S	T	W	I	A	Ld
Spearman	4	3	3	3	3	1	3	1	7
Sergeant	4	3	3	3	3	1	3	2	7

UNIT SIZE: 10+

EQUIPMENT: Hand weapon, spear, light armour.

SPECIAL RULES:
State Troops.

OPTIONS:
- Any unit may be equipped with shields for +1 pt/per model.
- Upgrade one Spearman to a musician for +4 pts.
- Upgrade one Spearman to a standard bearer for +8 pts.
- Promote one Spearman to a Sergeant for +8 pts.

SWORDSMEN

Points/model: 6

	M	WS	BS	S	T	W	I	A	Ld
Swordsman	4	4	3	3	3	1	4	1	7
Duellist	4	4	3	3	3	1	4	2	7

UNIT SIZE: 10+

EQUIPMENT: Sword (hand weapon), light armour and shield.

SPECIAL RULES
State Troops.

OPTIONS:
- Upgrade one Swordsman to a musician for +5 pts.
- Upgrade one Swordsman to a standard bearer for +10 pts.
- Promote one Swordsman to a Duellist for +10 pts.

KNIGHTLY ORDERS

Points/model: 23

	M	WS	BS	S	T	W	I	A	Ld
Knight	4	4	3	3	3	1	3	1	8
Preceptor	4	4	3	3	3	1	3	2	8
Warhorse	8	3	–	3	3	1	3	1	5

UNIT SIZE: 5+

MOUNT: Barded Warhorse.

EQUIPMENT: Hand weapon, full plate armour. Knights may be armed with either a lance and a shield, or a great weapon. (Note that Knights of the White Wolf may be armed with a mix of cavalry hammers and great hammers. For game purposes, they are all considered to be armed with great weapons.)

OPTIONS:
- Upgrade one Knight to a musician for +8 pts.
- Upgrade one Knight to a standard bearer for +16 pts.
- Promote one Knight to a Preceptor for +16 pts.
- A standard bearer may carry a magic standard worth up to 50 points.

ARMY ORGANISATION:
Knights of the Inner Circle: You may upgrade any unit of Knights to be Inner Circle Knights at a cost of +3 points per model. Units of Inner Circle Knights (including the Preceptor) have Strength 4. They count as a Special Units choice rather than a Core Units choice.

CORE UNITS

HANDGUNNERS

Points/model: 8

	M	WS	BS	S	T	W	I	A	Ld
Handgunner	4	3	3	3	3	1	3	1	7
Marksman	4	3	4	3	3	1	3	1	7

UNIT SIZE: 10+

EQUIPMENT: Handgun, hand weapon.

SPECIAL RULES:
State Troops.

OPTIONS:

• Upgrade one Handgunner to a musician for +5 pts.

• Upgrade one Handgunner to a standard bearer for +10 pts.

• Promote one Handgunner to a Marksman for +5 pts.

• The Marksman may carry one of the following weapons instead of his handgun: Hochland long rifle (+20pts); repeater handgun (+15pts); brace of pistols (free).

CROSSBOWMEN

Points/model: 8

	M	WS	BS	S	T	W	I	A	Ld
Crossbowman	4	3	3	3	3	1	3	1	7
Marksman	4	3	4	3	3	1	3	1	7

UNIT SIZE: 10+

EQUIPMENT: Crossbow, hand weapon.

SPECIAL RULES:
State Troops.

OPTIONS:

• Upgrade one Crossbowman to a musician for +5 pts.

• Upgrade one Crossbowman to a standard bearer for +10 pts.

• Promote one Crossbowman to a Marksman for +5 pts.

ARCHERS

Points/model: 8

	M	WS	BS	S	T	W	I	A	Ld
Archer	4	3	3	3	3	1	3	1	7
Marksman	4	3	4	3	3	1	3	1	7

UNIT SIZE: 10-20

EQUIPMENT: Bow, hand weapon.

SPECIAL RULES
Militia; Skirmishers.

OPTIONS:

• Promote one Archer to a Marksman for +5 pts.

ARMY ORGANISATION

Huntsmen: A single unit of Archers may be upgraded to Huntsmen at a cost of +2 points/model. Huntsmen have the Scouts special rule.

FREE COMPANY

Points/model: 5

	M	WS	BS	S	T	W	I	A	Ld
Fighter	4	3	3	3	3	1	3	1	7
Sergeant	4	3	3	3	3	1	3	2	7

UNIT SIZE: 10+

EQUIPMENT: Free Companies are armed with a variety of weapons. However, for game purposes they are all considered to be armed with two hand weapons.

SPECIAL RULES:
Militia.

OPTIONS:

• Upgrade one Fighter to a musician for +4 pts.

• Upgrade one Fighter to a standard bearer for +8 pts.

• Promote one Fighter to a Sergeant for +8 pts.

SPECIAL UNITS

GREATSWORDS

Points/model: 10

	M	WS	BS	S	T	W	I	A	Ld
Greatsword	4	4	3	3	3	1	3	1	8
Count's Champion	4	4	3	3	3	1	3	2	8

UNIT SIZE: 5+

EQUIPMENT: Two-handed sword (great weapon), hand weapon, full plate armour.

SPECIAL RULES:
Stubborn, State Troops.

OPTIONS:
- Upgrade one Greatsword to a musician for +6 pts.
- Upgrade one Greatsword to a standard bearer for +12 pts.
- Promote one Greatsword to a Count's Champion for +12 pts.

PISTOLIERS

Points/model: 18

	M	WS	BS	S	T	W	I	A	Ld
Pistolier	4	3	3	3	3	1	3	1	7
Outrider	4	3	4	3	3	1	3	1	7
Warhorse	8	3	–	3	3	1	3	1	5

UNIT SIZE: 5+

MOUNT: Warhorse.

EQUIPMENT: Brace of pistols, light armour.

SPECIAL RULES:
Fast Cavalry.

OPTIONS:
- Upgrade one Pistolier to a musician for +7 pts.
- Promote one Pistolier to an Outrider for +7 pts.
- An Outrider may exchange one of his pistols for a repeater pistol for +10 pts.

OUTRIDERS

Points/model: 21

	M	WS	BS	S	T	W	I	A	Ld
Outrider	4	3	4	3	3	1	3	1	7
Outrider Champion	4	3	5	3	3	1	3	1	7
Warhorse	8	3	–	3	3	1	3	1	5

UNIT SIZE: 5+

EQUIPMENT: Repeater handgun, hand weapon, light armour.

SPECIAL RULES:
Fast Cavalry

OPTIONS:
- Upgrade one Outrider to a musician for +8 pts.
- Promote one Outrider to an Outrider Champion for +16 pts.
- The Outrider Champion may carry one of the following weapons instead of his repeater handgun: repeater pistol and pistol (free), grenade launching blunderbuss (free), Hochland long rifle (+5 pts).
- Outriders may equip their Warhorses with barding for +2 points per model (Outriders on barded Warhorses no longer count as fast cavalry).

GREAT CANNON

Points/model: 100

	M	WS	BS	S	T	W	I	A	Ld
Great Cannon	–	–	–	–	7	3	–	–	–
Crewman	4	3	3	3	3	1	3	1	7

NUMBER OF CREW: 3

EQUIPMENT: Each crewman carries a hand weapon.

MORTAR

Points/model: 75

	M	WS	BS	S	T	W	I	A	Ld
Mortar	–	–	–	–	7	3	–	–	–
Crewman	4	3	3	3	3	1	3	1	7

NUMBER OF CREW: 3

EQUIPMENT: Each crewman carries a hand weapon.

RARE UNITS

FLAGELLANT WARBAND

Points/model: 10

	M	WS	BS	S	T	W	I	A	Ld
Flagellant	4	2	2	3	3	1	3	1	10
Prophet of Doom	4	2	2	3	3	1	3	2	10

UNIT SIZE: 5-30

EQUIPMENT: Flail.

SPECIAL RULES:
Unbreakable, Crazed!, The End is Nigh!

OPTIONS:
• Promote one Flagellant to a Prophet of Doom for +10 pts.

ARMY ORGANISATION:
If the army includes one or more Priests of Sigmar (Warrior Priests or Arch Lectors), you may include one (and only one) Flagellant Warband as a Core Units choice instead of Rare.

HELBLASTER VOLLEY GUN

Points/model: 110

	M	WS	BS	S	T	W	I	A	Ld
Volley Gun	–	–	–	–	7	3	–	–	–
Crewman	4	3	3	3	3	1	3	1	7

NUMBER OF CREW: 3

EQUIPMENT: Each crewman carries a hand weapon.

HELSTORM ROCKET BATTERY

Points/model: 115

	M	WS	BS	S	T	W	I	A	Ld
Rocket Battery	–	–	–	–	7	3	–	–	–
Crewman	4	3	3	3	3	1	3	1	7

NUMBER OF CREW: 3

EQUIPMENT: Each crewman carries a hand weapon.

STEAM TANK

Points/model: 300

	M	WS	BS	S	T	W	I	A	Ld
Steam Tank	special	–	–	6	6	10	–	special	–
Engineer Commander	–	–	4	–	–	–	–	–	10

UNIT SIZE: 1

ARMOUR SAVE: 1+

EQUIPMENT: Main cannon and steam gun. The Engineer Commander carries a repeater pistol.

SPECIAL RULES:
Large Target, Unbreakable, Terror, Unit Strength 10.

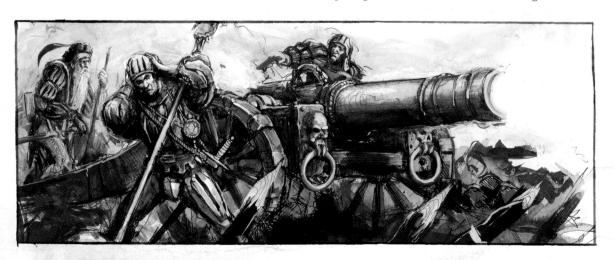

SUMMARY

LORDS	M	WS	BS	S	T	W	I	A	Ld	Special Rules	Page
Arch Lector	4	4	3	4	4	3	4	2	9	Blessings of Sigmar, Righteous Fury, Prayers of Sigmar	52
Balthasar Gelt	4	3	3	3	4	3	3	1	8	Alchemist Supreme	64
Emperor Karl Franz	4	6	5	4	4	3	6	4	10	Leader of Men, Deathclaw	56
General of the Empire	4	5	5	4	4	3	5	3	9		34
Grand Theogonist	4	5	3	4	4	3	4	2	9	Grand Theogonist, Aura of Righteousness, Frenzy.	60
Kurt Helborg	4	7	3	4	4	3	6	4	9	The Emperor's Chosen	58
Templar Grand Master	4	6	3	4	4	3	6	4	9	Master of Battle	40
Wizard Lord	4	3	3	3	4	3	3	1	8		44

HEROES	M	WS	BS	S	T	W	I	A	Ld	Special Rules	Page
Battle Wizard	4	3	3	3	3	2	3	1	7		44
Captain of the Empire	4	5	5	4	4	2	5	3	8		34
Ludwig Schwarzhelm	4	6	5	4	4	2	5	3	8	The Emperor's Standard, Killing Blow, Bodyguard	59
Luthor Huss	4	5	3	4	4	2	4	2	8	Warrior Priest, The Chosen of Sigmar, Cause Fear	62
Master Engineer	4	3	4	3	3	2	3	1	7	Master of Ballistics, Extra Crewman	46
Warrior Priest	4	4	3	4	4	2	4	2	8	Blessings of Sigmar, Righteous Fury, Prayers of Sigmar	52

TROOPS	M	WS	BS	S	T	W	I	A	Ld	Special Rules	Page
Archer	4	3	3	3	3	1	3	1	7	Militia, Skirmishers	37
Crewman	4	3	3	3	3	1	3	1	7		
Crossbowman	4	3	3	3	3	1	3	1	7	State Troops	36
Flagellant	4	2	2	3	3	1	3	1	10	Unbreakable, Crazed!, The End is Nigh!	54
Free Company Fighter	4	3	3	3	3	1	3	1	7	Militia	36
Great Cannon	–	–	–	–	7	3	–	–	–		45
Greatsword	4	4	3	3	3	1	3	1	8	Stubborn, State Troops	43
Halberdier	4	3	3	3	3	1	3	1	7	State Troops	36
Handgunner	4	3	3	3	3	1	3	1	7	State Troops	36
Helblaster Volley Gun	–	–	–	–	7	3	–	–	–		48
Helstorm Rocket Battery	–	–	–	–	7	3	–	–	–		49
Knight	4	4	3	3	3	1	3	1	8		40
Knight of the Inner Circle	4	4	3	4	3	1	3	1	8		40
Spearman	4	3	3	3	3	1	3	1	7	State Troops	36
Swordsman	4	4	3	3	3	1	4	1	7	State Troops	36
Mortar	–	–	–	–	7	3	–	–	–		45
Outrider	4	3	4	3	3	1	3	1	7	Fast cavalry	42
Pistolier	4	3	3	3	3	1	3	1	7	Fast cavalry	42
Steam Tank	special	–	–	6	6	10	–	special	–	Large Target, Unbreakable, Terror, Unit Strength 10	50

MOUNTS	M	WS	BS	S	T	W	I	A	Ld	Special Rules	Page
Deathclaw	6	6	–	5	5	4	5	4	8	Fly, Terror, large target	56
Griffon	6	5	–	5	5	4	5	4	7	Fly, Terror, large target	35
The Imperial Dragon	6	6	–	6	6	6	3	5	8	Fly, Terror, large target, S4 flaming breath weapon, scaly skin (3+)	35
Imperial Pegasus	8	3	–	4	4	3	4	2	6	Fly	35
The War Altar	–	–	–	5	5	5	–	–	–	Large Target, Unit Strength 5, Golden Griffon, The Power of Sigmar	53
Warhorse	8	3	–	3	3	1	3	1	5		35

Original Book: Rick Priestley. **Cover Art:** David Gallagher. **Illustration:** John Blanche, Alex Boyd, Paul Dainton, David Gallagher, Karl Kopinski, Ian Miller & Adrian Smith. **Graphic Design:** Pete Borlace & Alun Davies. **Miniatures Sculptors:** Tim Adcock, Mike Anderson, Colin Grayson, Alex Hedström, Aly Morrison, Brian Nelson, Alan Perry, Michael Perry, Steve Saleh & Dave Thomas. **'Eavy Metal:** Fil Dunn, Pete Foley, Neil Green, Neil Langdown, Darren Latham, Keith Robertson, Anja Wettergren & Kirsten Williams. **Hobby Material:** Dave Andrews, Neil Hodgson, Mark Jones, Chad Mierzwa, Dominic Murray & Adrian Wood. **Production:** Michelle Barson, Marc Elliott, Dylan Owen, Mark Owen, Mark Raynor, Ian Strickland, Sean Turtle & Nathan Winter. **Special Thanks To:** The Geeks play-testers, Mat Ward, Graham Davey, Jeremy Vetock & Alan Merrett.

UK	US	Canada	Australia	Northern Europe
Games Workshop Ltd., Willow Rd, Lenton, Nottingham. NG7 2WS	Games Workshop Inc., 6711 Baymeadow Drive, Glen Burnie, Maryland 21060-6401	Games Workshop, 2679 Bristol Circle, Unit 3, Oakville, Ontario, L6H 6Z8	Games Workshop, 23 Liverpool Street, Ingleburn NSW 2565	Games Workshop Ltd., Willow Rd, Lenton, Nottingham. NG7 2WS, UK

THE EMPIRE ARMY

There are many different approaches when painting an Empire force. A popular method is to create an army from a particular State. Alternatively you can build a force that combines regiments from all over the Empire. This final section of the book shows these options, as well as individual models and units, plus a guide to the various State colours.

The State regiments of this Empire army bear the red and white livery of Talabheim.

This Empire force has regiments from different States, as well as two Knightly Orders and a Flagellant Warband.

HEROES OF THE EMPIRE

Karl Franz may
choose to wield
a runefang.

▲ **Emperor Karl Franz**
riding his loyal Griffon
Deathclaw, one of the
many mounts housed in
the Imperial zoo

▲ **Ludwig Schwarzhelm**
The Emperor's Champion

▲ **Middenheim Captain**
with great hammer

▲ **Empire General**
from Wissenland

▲ **Marius Leitdorf**
The mad Elector Count of Averlan

▲ **Valmir von Raukov**
Elector Count of Ostland,
defender of the northern Empire

▲ **Empire General**
from Talabheim, city of the comet

▲ **Boris Todbringer**
Elector Count of
Middenland, scourge of
the Drakwald Beastmen

▲ **Aldebrand Ludenhof**
Elector Count of Hochland

▲ **Empire General**
in full plate armour

▲ **Talabecland Captain**
with pistol

▲ **Battle Standard Bearer**
of the army of Reikland

STATE TROOPS

▲ Talabheim Sergeant

▲ **Halberdier Regiment**
Veterans of Nordland's battles
against Norse pirates

▲ Wissenland Spearman

▲ Swordsman from Ostland

▲ Hochland Handgunner

▲ Crossbowman from
the rustic Eastern
state of Stirland

▲ Swordsman of the
Stirland River Patrol

▲ Averland Crossbowman

▲ Swordsman clad in the
colours of Altdorf, the
Empire's richest city.

▽ **Handgunner Regiment**
from Nuln, home of the
Imperial Gunnery School

▲ Standard Bearer

MILITIA

▲ Huntsman

▲ **Free Company**
from Talabheim

▲ Middenheim
Fighter

▲ Talabecland
Fighter

▲ Militia
Sergeant

▲ Sergeant with
Warhammer

▲ Reikland
Sergeant

A Talabheim Halberdier regiment with Swordsman and Handgunner detachments

KNIGHTLY ORDERS

◄ Reiksguard Knights
Personal retinue of the
Emperor Karl Franz

A Preceptor
leads the regiment

The Reiksguard
bear symbols of
the Emperor on
their shields.

**► Knights of the
Blazing Sun**
This order wears
shining black and
gold armour.

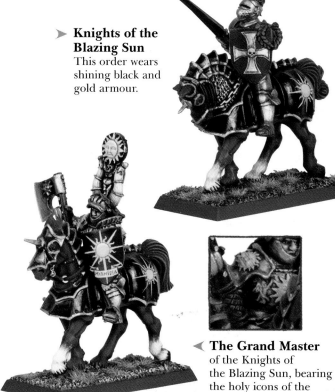

▲ Kurt Helborg
The Grand Master of the Reiksguard

The Solland Runefang,
finally returned to the
Empire many long
years after it was
captured by Gorbad
Ironclaw at the Battle
of Solland's Crown.

◄ The Grand Master
of the Knights of
the Blazing Sun, bearing
the holy icons of the
Arabyan Goddess Myrmidia

Knights of the White Wolf
Cloaked in the wolf pelts beloved of the warrior God Ulric

The Grand Master
of the Knights of the White Wolf, armed with a great hammer

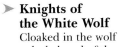

Knights Panther
This knightly order was founded during the crusades against Araby.

The Grand Master
of the Knights Panther

The Knights Panther have taken images of the exotic beasts of Araby as their heraldry and use pelts as cloaks and trophies.

ARTILLERY

Mortar
with crew in the colours of Talabheim.

Great Cannon
Mainstay of Empire artillery trains

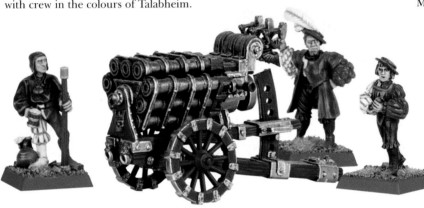

◁ **Helblaster Volley Gun**
The deadliest creation of
the College of Engineers

Helstorm Rocket Battery
Legacy of the eccentric Engineer
Herman Faulkstein

Master Engineer
with repeater handgun and
mounted on mechanical steed

Master Engineer
with repeater pistol

Master Engineer
with shoulder-slung
repeater handgun

Master Engineer
with Hochland
long rifle

PISTOLIERS AND OUTRIDERS

► **Pistoliers**
Hot-headed young
nobles, eager for battle

► **Outriders**
Grizzled veterans who have
survived their days as
pistoliers and learned to
master deadlier weaponry

▲ **Pistolier Musician**

▲ **Outrider Champion**

STEAM TANK

The heraldry of
the College of
Engineers,
complete with
the year of this
Steam Tank's
construction.

Steam gauges,
workings and
controls

GREATSWORDS

▲ Greatswords Regiment
from Talabheim

▲ Count's
Champion

▲ Averland
Greatsword

▲ Middenheim
Greatsword

▲ Carroburg
Greatsword

FLAGELLANT WARBAND

▲ Flagellants go into
battle convinced the
end of the world is
upon them.

WARRIOR PRIESTS OF SIGMAR

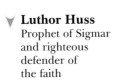

Luthor Huss
Prophet of Sigmar
and righteous
defender of
the faith

▼ Warrior Priest
with hand
weapon and
shield

▲ Warrior Priest with
two hand weapons

▲ Warrior Priest
with great
weapon and a
Holy Relic

▲ This Warrior Priest
bears a Sigil of Sigmar
upon his shield.

BATTLE WIZARDS

Vials of Al-kahest
can sear the flesh
of any foe

▲ Wizard of the
Bright Order

▲ Wizard Lord from
the College of Light

Balthasar Gelt
Supreme Patriarch of the
Colleges of Magic and
master of alchemy

▲ Wizard of the Grey College
with a Wizard's Staff

▲ Wizard of the
Celestial Order

COLOURS OF THE EMPIRE

The State Regiments of the Empire are disciplined, professional soldiers who train for war every day of their lives. Each province and city-state raises and trains its own soldiers at the expense of the Elector Count or Burgomeister and these are traditionally outfitted in the colours of their homeland.

There is great variation in styles – regiments hailing from the same province or town can look wildly different and even individuals within regiments tend to sport a range of patterns. These pages show some examples of State Troops from the various provinces of the Empire.

Ostermark – The rural people of the Ostermark are earthy, capable folk who often fight alongside the Kislevites in battles against the northern barbarians.

Talabecland – The state of Talabecland lies in the heart of the Empire and its armies often comprise small, elite forces of highly experienced soldiers.

Altdorf – As the largest and richest city in the Empire, the soldiers of Altdorf wear the most ostentatious clothing and carry the best weapons of all State Troops.

Ostland – The State Troops of Ostland are amongst the toughest and most stubborn in the Empire, hence the adoption of the bull as its symbol.

Middenheim – Clad in cold white and blue, the soldiers from the City of the White Wolf are burly, northern men who follow the creed of Ulric, god of winter, war and wolves.

Hochland – The people of Hochland are famed for hunting in the dense forests of their homeland, and a high proportion of its armies are made up of deadly accurate Handgunners.

Wissenland – The province of Wissenland has changed hands many times over the years and this has resulted in State Troops that are fiercely independent and train especially hard.

Nordland – The state of Nordland is sparsely populated and its regiments spend much of their time patrolling the coastline and defending their settlements against Norse raiders.

Nuln – Famous for the Imperial School of Gunnery, Nuln's soldiers commonly wear black uniforms to hide the ubiquitous soot stains from the many artillery pieces they fight alongside.

Averland – One of the wealthiest provinces in the Empire, thanks to its much sought after steeds, Averland's army is famous for its heavily ornamented uniforms.

Middenland – This is a desolate province of unforgiving climate and the impenetrable Drakwald Forest. The soldiers of this harsh land favour the god Ulric over Sigmar.

Talabheim – The great crater wall surrounding Talabheim requires a thousands-strong garrison to man. Those honoured with this duty wear the comet symbol on their livery.

Reikland (inc. Carroburg) – The Reikland is a large, wealthy and populous province. Its state colour is white, though some regiments, like the infamous Carroburg Greatswords, have developed their own heraldic traditions (see page 43).

Stirland – Stirland has a reputation as being a poor, rustic backwater and its soldiers are often equipped with simpler weapons. However, the Stirland Huntsmen are renowned throughout the Empire.

AN EMPIRE ARMY

This Empire army has been chosen to a total of 2,000 points, a common size of army for Warhammer battles, and painted to represent a force from the city of Talabheim. The core of the army consists of solid blocks of State Troops and their detachments, Greatswords and Flagellants, backed up by fast moving Pistoliers and a hard-hitting regiment of Knights. The addition of a General of the Empire, a Captain of the Empire and a Warrior Priest means the army will be hard to break. The Cannon and Mortar will pound the enemy from afar, forcing them to close with the Empire battle line, where the Helblaster Volley Gun will wreak havoc upon the enemy units.

1 Flagellant Warband   **210 pts**
This is a regiment of 20 Flagellants with flails.
The regiment has a Prophet of Doom.

2 Greatswords   **230 pts**
This is a regiment of 20 Greatswords with full plate armour and two-handed weapons. The regiment has a Count's Champion, a standard bearer and a musician.

3 Pistoliers   **114 pts**
This is a regiment of 5 Pistoliers, each armed with a brace of pistols. The regiment has a musician and an Outrider armed with a repeater pistol.

4 Bruno Schepke, Warrior Priest of Sigmar   **98 pts**
Bruno wears heavy armour and carries a two-handed hammer.

5 **Master Engineer Otto von Ritterberg**   **100 pts**
Otto is mounted on a mechanical steed and is equipped
with a hand weapon and a Repeater pistol.

6 **Crossbowmen**   **80 pts**
This is a detachment of 10 Crossbowmen attached to the
Swordsmen.

7 **Swordsmen**   **145 pts**
This is a unit of 20 Swordsmen in light armour with
shields and hand weapons. The regiment has a Duellist,
a standard bearer and a musician.

8 **Cannon**   **100 pts**

9 **Mortar**   **75 pts**

10 **Helblaster Volley Gun**   **110 pts**

11 **Markus Schiller, Captain**   **83 pts**
Markus is a Captain of the Empire and carries the battle
standard. He has a hand weapon and full plate armour.

12 **Albrecht von Krieghaus, Empire General**   **184 pts**
Mounted on a barded warhorse, Albrecht wears Gilded
Armour and carries a shield and the Sword of Power.

13 **Reiksguard Knights**   **270 pts**
This is a regiment of 10 Reiksguard Knights mounted on
barded warhorses. They are equipped with full plate
armour, shields, hand weapons and lances. The regiment
has a Preceptor, standard bearer and musician.

14 **Halberdiers**   **120 pts**
This is a unit of 20 Halberdiers in light armour with
halberds. The regiment has a Sergeant, musician and a
standard bearer.

15 **Handgunners**   **80 pts**
This is a detachment of 10 Handgunners attached to the
Halberdiers.